WeightWatchers®

The *Complete* Meal

Your ultimate guide to meal planning and cooking for weight loss

Welcome

The Complete Meal has everything you need to cook simple, delicious meals while losing weight.

This book is an essential companion to the ***ProPoints®* Plan**, the easy weight-loss programme that helps you choose the right foods, satisfy your hunger and keep you healthy. Inside we'll show you how simple it is to make your meals balanced, portion-controlled and, most importantly, absolutely delicious.

We start by revealing how to make the most of **Filling & Healthy Foods** – those reliable favourites you can turn to again and again to fill you up without weighing you down (see p9). When you're ready you can try a **Filling & Healthy Day** (see p25) to enjoy lots of these foods without needing to track ***ProPoints*** values.

We also share the simple steps to creating balanced meals that give you all the nutrients you need each day (see p12). If you're learning correct portion sizes, you'll love our handy tips and visual guides to healthy serving sizes (see p17).

One of the easiest ways to change eating habits is to make simple swaps. This way you can still enjoy the food and flavours you love while you're losing weight (see p18). There's also a quick quiz (see p22) and our indispensable guides to what food and equipment you need to get cooking (see p152 and 154).

With all this information you'll be well on the way to creating your own 'complete meals'. But if you still need a little help or a bit of inspiration, we have that covered, too. Our seasonal meal ideas (see p26), tasty recipes (see p34) and snack suggestions (see p148) will ensure *The Complete Meal* is never far from your kitchen!

KATE CODY
Director Publishing & Programme

Contents

Delicious & healthy cooking made easy

EATING THE RIGHT TYPES OF FOODS IN THE RIGHT AMOUNTS TO LOSE WEIGHT IS EASY ONCE YOU KNOW HOW.

Can you imagine a life without chocolate and other treats? No, neither can we. Fortunately you don't have to thanks to the *ProPoints Plan* – a flexible weight-loss programme that means you can still enjoy the foods you love and occasional treats. We believe weight loss works best when it fits around your life – not the other way around – so with this plan you can enjoy a wide variety of foods and confidently say "yes" to last-minute dinner invitations.

The secret is to focus on making healthy and balanced food choices most of the time, so when friends invite you for coffee and cake you can enjoy that chocolate brownie, knowing you've got it covered within your *ProPoints* budget.

Our meal ideas (see p26) and recipes (see p34) make losing weight easy because we've worked it all out for you. But because life is full of surprises and meals don't always come with *ProPoints* attached, we also want to show you how easy it is to plan your own meals based on **Filling & Healthy Foods** (see opposite). It's a balanced and delicious way of eating that will quickly become the way you love to eat. Here are four simple steps that will help you stay on track with your everyday food choices so you can lose weight and feel great.

To stay healthy and function at your best, you need to eat a wide variety of nutritious foods. Both our **Filling & Healthy Foods** (see Step 1, below) and Good Health Guidelines (see Step 2, p12) can help you here. **Filling & Healthy Foods** tell you which foods to focus on, while the Good Health Guidelines tell you the minimum serves you need to eat in each food group. Think of them as the food team that will help you lose weight and become familiar with what balanced healthy eating looks like and tastes like. Give your body the best foods and you'll love losing weight.

"If you need a snack, grab a piece of fruit – fruit is Filling & Healthy, plus it has 0 *ProPoints* values too." KATE CODY, DIRECTOR PUBLISHING & PROGRAMME

and sugar. We rank all foods within categories using a proprietary formula – those that rank best are deemed **Filling & Healthy Foods**, so make the most of them whenever you can. They are highlighted with a green triangle ▲ in all of our recipes and meal ideas, or use our easy reference table (see p10).

How do they work?

Many **Filling & Healthy Foods** are lower in energy density. That means they're bulky foods that are low in *ProPoints* values compared to their weight. Most people tend to eat the same amount of food each day regardless of the type of food. By replacing higher-kilojoule foods with low energy-dense **Filling & Healthy Foods** you can fill up your stomach and stay satisfied for fewer *ProPoints* values. This helps you to S-T-R-E-T-C-H your daily *ProPoints* allowance and your weekly *ProPoints* budget further.

Some **Filling & Healthy Foods** are also high in protein, which adds to a feeling of fullness. Try to eat plenty of **Filling & Healthy Foods** every day and you'll be healthier and keep the hunger pangs at bay.

1 CHOOSE FILLING & HEALTHY FOODS

At the centre of the *ProPoints* Plan are our **Filling & Healthy Foods**. They are the 'best of the best', selected because they're great for your weight loss and your health. They're filling because they're low in energy density and/or contain protein. They're healthy because they're high in fibre and/or low in saturated fat, salt

BY REPLACING HIGHER-KILOJOULE FOODS WITH FILLING & HEALTHY FOODS YOU CAN S-T-R-E-T-C-H YOUR *ProPoints* FURTHER.

Filling & healthy foods

PROTEIN

✓ **BEEF, PORK, VEAL, LAMB, CHICKEN AND TURKEY** – lean cuts, fat trimmed, all skin removed (refer to food list in your *Pocket Guide* for specific cuts).

✓ **GAME MEATS** – venison, kangaroo, goat, rabbit, buffalo and emu.

✓ **ORGAN MEATS** – beef, lamb and veal heart and kidney, plus lamb brains.

✓ **FISH AND SHELLFISH** – fresh, frozen or canned in springwater (see exceptions, below).

✓ **MEAT SUBSTITUTES** – including tofu and Quorn mince and pieces.

✓ **EGGS.**

✓ **DRIED AND CANNED BEANS** – including black, cannellini, red kidney, borlotti and fat-free refried beans.

✓ **DRIED PEAS** – including split peas, black-eyed peas and chickpeas.

✓ **LENTILS.**

NOT INCLUDED:

✗ **PROCESSED MEATS** – such as ham, bacon and hot dogs.

✗ **FISH AND SHELLFISH** – canned in oil or brine, plus fresh, frozen or canned red salmon, trout, ocean trout, perch, kingfish, gemfish, milkfish or yellow tail.

✗ **MEAT, POULTRY OR FISH** – with crumbs or added fat.

GRAINS

✓ **PASTA AND NOODLES** – unfilled wholemeal or other wholegrain only, such as wholemeal spaghetti or soba noodles.

✓ **RICE** – brown or wild only.

✓ **POPCORN** – air-popped, no added fat or salt.

✓ **GRAINS** – including, buckwheat, burghul (cracked wheat), polenta (cornmeal), rolled oats, pearl barley and quinoa.

✓ **CEREALS, HOT** – such as oatmeal/oat porridge (made with water or skim milk), without added sugar, dried fruits or nuts.

✓ **CEREALS, READY TO EAT** – wholegrain with 4g fibre or more per serving (such as puffed wheat, wheat biscuits and wheat flakes) and no added sugar, sugar coating, dried fruits or nuts.

✓ **CRISPBREAD** – Ryvita (multigrain or rye) or Kavli Crispy Thin.

NOT INCLUDED:

✗ **BREAD** – all types, including wholegrain.

✗ **BREADCRUMBS** – all types.

✗ **NOODLES WITH FLAVOUR SACHETS.**

DAIRY

✓ **SKIM MILK.**

✓ **LOW-FAT COTTAGE CHEESE.**

✓ **DIET FLAVOURED YOGHURT** – no added muesli or dried fruit.

✓ **LOW-FAT NATURAL YOGHURT** – no added muesli or dried fruit.

✓ **MILK SUBSTITUTE** – rice milk and unflavoured low-fat, reduced-fat or calcium-fortified soy.

NOT INCLUDED:

✗ **FLAVOURED MILK AND DRINKING YOGHURT.**

✗ **BUTTERMILK, ICE-CREAM AND HARD CHEESE.**

FRUIT & VEGETABLES

✓ **ALL FRESH, FROZEN AND CANNED FRUIT** – in natural juice and without added sugar.

✓ **ALL FRESH, FROZEN OR CANNED VEGETABLES** – without added sugar, flavourings or oil.

✓ **POTATOES** – all types.

NOT INCLUDED:

✗ **CANNED FRUIT** – in syrup.

✗ **DRIED FRUITS.**

✗ **FRUIT JUICES.**

✗ **AVOCADOS.**

✗ **OLIVES.**

✗ **POTATO CHIPS AND FRIES.**

✗ **PICKLED FOODS** – such as gherkins.

Fill me up fast

It's easy to make your meals more satisfying with **Filling & Healthy Foods**. Simply base your meals and snacks on a variety of **Filling & Healthy Foods**, then add your other favourite ingredients and flavours.

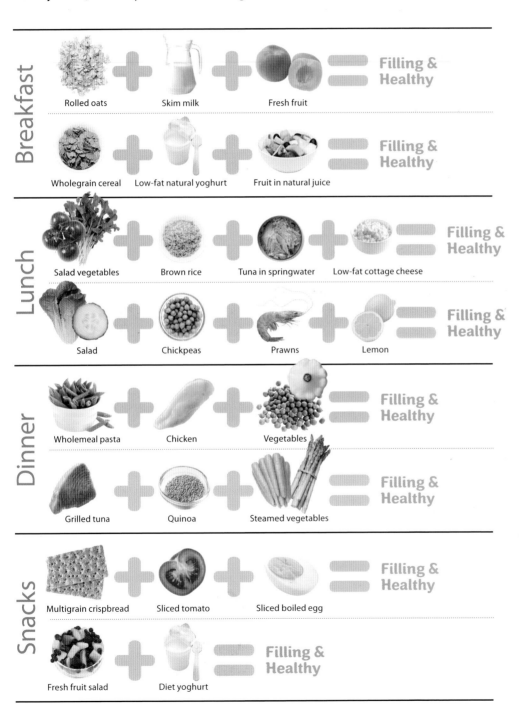

Breakfast

Rolled oats + Skim milk + Fresh fruit = Filling & Healthy

Wholegrain cereal + Low-fat natural yoghurt + Fruit in natural juice = Filling & Healthy

Lunch

Salad vegetables + Brown rice + Tuna in springwater + Low-fat cottage cheese = Filling & Healthy

Salad + Chickpeas + Prawns + Lemon = Filling & Healthy

Dinner

Wholemeal pasta + Chicken + Vegetables = Filling & Healthy

Grilled tuna + Quinoa + Steamed vegetables = Filling & Healthy

Snacks

Multigrain crispbread + Sliced tomato + Sliced boiled egg = Filling & Healthy

Fresh fruit salad + Diet yoghurt = Filling & Healthy

TRY TO EAT MORE WHOLEGRAINS

While not all wholegrain foods are classed as **Filling & Healthy Foods** (such as wholegrain or multigrain bread), they are still a better choice as they keep you feeling fuller for longer than more highly processed carbohydrates. They are also higher in fibre, which is better for your health and digestion.

You should try to eat wholegrains whenever you can. Here's how:

- Swap white pasta with wholemeal pasta.
- Enjoy one of the many multigrain breads, including soy and linseed, rye and spelt.
- Replace white bread, rolls, pita and crumpets with wholegrain or wholemeal varieties.
- Look for recipes with oats or oatmeal.
- Top yoghurt with oats or muesli.
- In recipes, switch half the white flour with wholemeal flour.
- Snack on air-popped plain popcorn (it's a wholegrain).
- Include wholegrain crackers and crispbreads as snacks.
- Try brown rice instead of white rice.
- Substitute quinoa for couscous.

AIM FOR BALANCE 2

According to Weight Watchers Good Health Guidelines, each day you should aim to eat:

- One to two serves* of protein (lean meat and poultry, fish, seafood, eggs, beans, lentils, nuts, seeds and tofu).
- Wholegrains whenever you can (bread, pasta, breakfast cereals, soba noodles and grains such as brown rice and oats).

- Two serves of dairy (milk, cream, cheese, yoghurt and non-dairy substitutes).
- Two serves of fruit.
- Five serves of vegetables.
- Two teaspoons of healthy oils (from olive, safflower, canola, sunflower and linseed/flaxseed oils).

Focus on eating the serves recommended by these guidelines and you'll feel satisfied after every meal and less likely to snack.

If you combine this know-how with healthier cooking methods (such as poaching, steaming or grilling) and cut down on sugary and fatty foods it will help you lose weight. Then when you do treat yourself to a slice of chocolate cake, you can enjoy it knowing it fits within your overall *ProPoints* budget, and that you're getting the balance right by favouring healthy foods.

*For what equals a serve, see Step 3, p16.

Protein

Wholegrains

Dairy

Healthy oils

Fruit

Vegetables

Eat a rainbow

Did you know different kinds of fruit and vegies provide different amounts and types of nutrients to each other? So for maximum health and protection against disease you need to eat a wide variety. Aim to eat five kinds of vegetables and two kinds of fruit every day for good health, and to make your meals more interesting. Foods of similar colours often contain the same type of nutrients (eg red foods such as tomatoes and watermelon both contain lycopene – which is thought to have anti-cancer properties) so try to eat a 'rainbow' of foods every day (see right).

Fruit and vegies – your 0 *ProPoints* friends!

All fruit and vegetables are **Filling & Healthy Foods**, and all fruit and most vegies also have 0 *ProPoints* values. This makes them great for snacking or for bulking up meals and desserts without using your daily *ProPoints* allowance. Of course, all foods have kilojoules, but we've already calculated them into your daily *ProPoints* allowance so you can confidently eat 0 *ProPoints* value fruit and vegies without affecting your weight-loss goals. Use your hunger and satisfaction signals as a guide and stop eating at 'just right', not 'full'.

DURING YOUR 'RAINBOW' DAY YOU MIGHT EAT:
RED: Strawberries or rhubarb on your porridge for breakfast or tomatoes with your eggs.
ORANGE: Carrot sticks or pawpaw for morning tea.
YELLOW & GREEN: Corn on the cob, button squash, snow peas and mixed salad leaves for lunch.
BLUE/INDIGO: Blueberries or plums for dessert or a snack.
VIOLET/WHITE: Eggplant, cabbage, cauliflower or potatoes as side dishes at dinner.

LOVE YOUR VEGIES

Go beyond meat and three veg. There are lots of clever ways to load up on vegies while you work towards five serves a day. Try these tricks:

1 *Add grated carrot and zucchini to rissoles, bolognaise sauce, or a shepherd's or cottage pie.*

2 *Try grated beetroot for extra bulk and flavour in Mexican beef and beans.*

3 *Whizz chopped onion, carrot, celery and zucchini in your food processor to use as a base for casseroles.*

4 *Vegies can also be added to sweet dishes such as zucchini and carrot cake or pumpkin scones.*

5 *Add mushrooms, spinach or tomatoes to scrambled eggs.*

Getting your daily dairy

RESEARCH SHOWS DAIRY CAN HELP WITH WEIGHT LOSS BECAUSE IT FILLS YOU UP FOR FEWER KILOJOULES.

Many of us are at risk of not having enough calcium in our diets, which increases the possibility of osteoporosis as we age. Some loss of calcium is inevitable as we grow older, so whether you are male or female it is important to build up good calcium stores when you are young and maintain them throughout your life.

Dairy and weight loss

The easiest way to get your calcium is by eating a minimum of two serves of dairy each day. Unfortunately, when people want to lose weight they often believe that dairy is 'bad' for weight loss, and therefore stop eating it. However, research shows that dairy can help with weight loss because its low energy density and high protein content makes it especially filling. As a bonus, by choosing low-fat or no-fat dairy products you're actually boosting your calcium intake at the same time as aiding your weight loss.

LACTOSE INTOLERANT?

Getting enough daily calcium is still important if you are lactose intolerant. Dairy products labelled 'lactose free' are one way, or try alternatives such as calcium-enriched soy milk. Other strategies include:

- Consume small amounts of milk (eg ½ cup or less) or other dairy foods at a time (so your body isn't overloaded).
- Try yoghurt with live acidophilus and bifidus cultures (digestion reduces its lactose content).
- Add lactase drops to milk or use lactase pills.

If you can't tolerate milk or yoghurt, try aged hard cheese (eg cheddar) as more than half the lactose is removed by the ageing process. Otherwise, consider a calcium supplement and look for calcium-fortified foods such as orange juice, cereal or bread. Other good sources of calcium are tofu processed with calcium sulphate, canned sardines or salmon with bones.

NOTE: Although dried beans and leafy greens (eg spinach) contain calcium, they also contain substances that interfere with calcium absorption.

5 EASY WAYS TO ADD CALCIUM

1 *Use 1 cup of skim milk on your cereal and in hot drinks, such as hot chocolate.*

2 *Use 1 cup skim milk to make a smoothie – try blending with banana, yoghurt and a drizzle of honey.*

3 *Keep tubs of low-fat or diet yoghurt in the fridge and eat it by itself, with fruit, or poured over cereal.*

4 *Sprinkle your pasta dishes with a little parmesan or reduced-fat cheddar cheese.*

5 *For a quick and creamy pasta sauce, mix reduced-fat evaporated milk with 1–2 tbs cornflour.*

Which fats & oils are OK?

You need to include some fats in your diet – the key is knowing which ones.

Healthy fats

Healthy fats – both monounsaturated and polyunsaturated – generally come from plant foods such as seeds (including canola, sunflower, safflower and linseed), olives, nuts, avocado, or oily fish (such as salmon and sardines). They can help lower blood cholesterol and are a good source of the disease-fighting antioxidant vitamin E. However, too much of any fat will cause weight gain so eat it in moderation. Aim for two teaspoons of healthy oils a day, which can be used for:

- cooking (such as roasting or chargrilling);
- making salad dressing;
- drizzling over vegies, soup or pasta.

Unhealthy fats

For good heart health you should reduce the amount of unhealthy saturated fat you are eating. Most saturated fat comes from animal products and the main culprits are:

- fried foods, chips and crisps;
- commercial biscuits, cakes and pastries;
- full-cream dairy products, such as milk, ice-cream, cream, butter and sour cream;
- fatty meats and processed meat, such as sausages, pork spare ribs, mid-loin chops, salami and mortadella.

Olive

Safflower

Canola

Linseed/flaxseed

Sunflower

TOP 5 OILS FOR GOOD HEALTH

To make it easy for you to pick the right oils, Weight Watchers has identified the top five healthy choices:

1 Canola.
2 Linseed/flaxseed.
3 Olive.
4 Safflower.
5 Sunflower.

CUT THE FAT

To limit your fat intake, try:

- using cooking oil spray when frying, roasting, barbecuing, grilling or greasing cake tins;
- water instead of oil when cooking onion;
- choosing lean cuts of meat, trimming fat from other cuts and removing skin from poultry.

CRUNCH TIME

Nuts and seeds provide a good mix of healthy fats, protein, vitamins and minerals. However they are high in kilojoules, so it's best to stick with one small handful a day and look up the *ProPoints* values first. Good choices include unsalted raw almonds, Brazil nuts, cashews, walnuts, pecans and pine nuts, as well as pepitas (pumpkin kernels), sunflower and sesame seeds.

3 WATCH PORTION SIZES

It's not just the type of food you eat that matters – even healthy food can make you gain weight if you eat too much of it. So if your steak hangs over the plate or your muffin looks like it's on steroids, then it's too big. You don't have to weigh everything but if you become familiar with correct portion sizes you'll be less likely to overeat. Just follow our easy reference guide (see below) and use the photos in our recipe chapters as a good visual guide to what correct portion sizes look like on a plate.

What is a serve?

PROTEIN	GRAINS	DAIRY	FRUIT & VEGETABLES
✓ 65–100g cooked lean meat or skinless poultry (such as ½ cup cooked lean mince, 2 small chops, or 2 slices roast meat).	✓ 2 slices (60g) wholemeal or multigrain bread.	✓ 1 cup skim, no-fat or low-fat milk.	✓ 2 small pieces of fruit (such as plums, apricots or fresh dates).
✓ 80–120g cooked fish fillet.	✓ 1 medium (50g) wholemeal or multigrain bread roll.	✓ ½ cup low-fat evaporated milk.	✓ 1 medium-sized piece of fruit (such as an apple, banana, orange or pear).
✓ 2 small eggs.	✓ 1 cup (180g) cooked rice, pasta or noodles.	✓ 200g tub diet or low-fat natural yoghurt.	✓ 1 small bunch of grapes.
✓ 100g tofu.	✓ 1 cup (230g) porridge.	✓ 30g reduced-fat hard cheese or feta.	✓ ½ punnet strawberries.
✓ ⅓ cup nuts.	✓ ⅓ cup (40g) breakfast cereal flakes.	✓ 100g low-fat cottage or ricotta cheese.	✓ ½ cup cooked vegetables.
✓ ¼ cup seeds (such as sesame, sunflower or pepitas [pumpkin kernels]).	✓ 2 wheat-flake or oat-flake breakfast biscuits.		✓ 1 small potato.
✓ ½ cup cooked legumes (such as lentils, chickpeas or red kidney or cannellini beans).	✓ ½ cup (65g) untoasted muesli.		✓ 1 cup salad vegetables.
	✓ ⅓ cup (40g) flour.		✓ ½ cup cooked legumes (such as chickpeas, lentils or kidney beans).

THE DIVIDED PLATE

You might be used to filling half your plate with protein, with the other half divided between vegies and carbohydrates (such as pasta or potato). But it's better to fill half the plate with non-starchy vegies and make one-quarter carbohydrates (such as grains) and starchy vegetables (such as potato, sweet potato, peas or corn), and the other quarter lean protein.

I medium bread roll or I cup pasta

½ cup cooked vegies or rice

Picture perfect

One of the best ways to judge portion sizes correctly is to compare them with everyday objects (see above and right). This way you'll create a 'visual memory' of how big things should be. As a general rule, don't eat anything much larger than your fist unless it is 0 *ProPoints* value vegetables or fruit.

100g cooked red meat or chicken

"To keep portion sizes in check, avoid using huge dinner plates. The recipe photographs in this book (from p34) are also a great guide to how correct portions should look."

KATE CODY, DIRECTOR PUBLISHING & PROGRAMME

DINING OUT

Going to restaurants or attending a dinner party is supposed to be fun, so don't let portion sizes get in the way of a good time. Here are some handy hints for keeping meal sizes in check when you're not in charge of the kitchen:

- Eat some 0 *ProPoints* value fruit or vegies before you leave home so you are less likely to overeat.
- Order an entree-size main meal and a side plate of vegetables or salad (ask them to hold the oil and place sauces or dressing on the side).
- Opt for shared meals where possible so you determine how much goes on your plate.
- Eat slowly so if your host offers you seconds you can politely decline.
- If you want to indulge, remember that's what your weekly *ProPoints* budget is for, so enjoy!

FAMILY MATTERS

Just because you're trying to lose weight doesn't mean you have to cook separate meals for the rest of the household. A larger protein portion or an extra serve of grains (such as bread) or starchy vegetables (think potato and sweet potato) will satisfy your partner or growing teens.

4 MAKE SIMPLE SWAPS

One way you can enjoy all your favourite foods and lose weight is to adopt a simple swap mindset. A passion for caramel lattes? Use skim rather than full-cream milk. Love pasta bakes? Then tweak your favourite recipe by using reduced-fat ingredients and healthier cooking methods (see our Lasagne, p105). When you add them all up, these small changes will make a big difference without feeling like a lot of hard work.

SWAP TO 'MINDFUL' EATING...CONCENTRATE ON THE DIFFERENT FLAVOURS/TEXTURES AND CHEW SLOWLY.

Practise 'mindful' eating

Ever noticed how quickly a bag of chips disappears when you're watching a movie? That's because your mind is somewhere else. When you pay more attention to what you eat you are less likely to overindulge. So swap mindless eating for 'mindful' eating. At work, try to eat away from your desk, while at home you should sit at the dinner table with the TV or computer off. As you eat, try to concentrate on the different flavours and textures of your meal and chew slowly – this gives your brain time to realise that you're full. And if you are engrossed in the latest blockbuster, choose small individual packets or place your serve in a different dish.

5 EATING HABITS TO SWAP

1 Sit at the table instead of in front of the TV. Research shows you will eat less when not distracted.

2 Put your fork down between mouthfuls and eat slowly instead of rushing your meals.

3 Instead of keeping your favourite treats at home, only eat them when you are out so they are less accessible.

4 Have something to drink before reaching for a snack. You may then find you don't need it.

5 Don't go cold turkey with your favourite foods – it may make you crave them more. Rather, limit how often you indulge.

6 ways to swap

T here are many ways to swap – you can swap the same amount of food for a healthier or lower *ProPoints* value alternative, swap to a down-sized portion, or a combination of all these things. It's completely up to you.

"One of the easiest swaps to make when cooking is to use spray oil instead of pouring it from a bottle." LUCY KELLY, SENIOR FOOD EDITOR

| White toast | Wholegrain toast | Large full-fat latte | Small skim-milk latte |

| Large chocolate bar | Small serve of your favourite | Eating chips from a large bowl or bag | Small individual packets or servings |

| Full-fat cheese | Reduced-fat varieties | Large serve/bowl of ice-cream | Small portion-controlled version |

Snack smart

Plan any snacks, rather than snack on auto-pilot, so you only have them when you really need them. If you're out and about and your regular meal times are affected it's handy to have something on hand. Tuck a healthy and low *ProPoints* value snack in your:

- car glovebox
- handbag
- desk drawer
- gym bag.

DECODING LABELS

Product labels can be confusing, so here's a simple guide:

LOW FAT: Can only be used to describe a product with less than three per cent fat.

REDUCED FAT: Has at least 25 per cent less fat than its full-fat equivalent but the fat content may still be quite high.

LITE OR LIGHT: Be careful, this may refer to the flavour, colour or even the weight of the item rather than the fat content.

SHOP TACTICS

Love it or not, supermarket shopping is so much easier if you follow these tips:

1 **Make a list:** To avoid unnecessary food purchases, write a list based on what you actually need rather than wandering around the aisles tossing in random 'what if' items. With a list you'll be surprised at how much less you buy and spend.

2 **Check your fridge and pantry:** Before you head out, find out what you already have so you avoid doubling up on ingredients, which can lead to food waste.

3 **Shop on a full stomach:** It's not just a myth – if you shop when you're hungry you're more likely to load up the trolley with food you don't need, and with less healthy options.

4 **Stay focused:** Stick to your list and don't be swayed by displays selling products you don't need. If it helps, pretend you're in a race to get through the checkouts in the quickest time possible.

5 **Beware bulk buys:** Bulk buying and two-for-one deals can save you money, however, it can sometimes make you eat more because there is an abundance of food. Limit bulk buys to things like toilet paper and food that you can freeze.

Making it work

You've read the theory, now see how easy it is to put our four simple steps into practice. We've selected three recipes from this book to show you what a day of eating balanced, portion-controlled meals might look like on your plate.

Creating balanced meals doesn't have to be an exact science. You don't always have to include all the daily serves recommended in our Good Health Guidelines in your three main meals – you won't find all your daily serves in the three meals shown here, though they give a useful guide to what a balanced meal looks like. Spread your serves across the whole day in any way that works

for you. For instance, you might boost your serves of dairy, fruit and vegetables by eating them as snacks throughout the day.

We believe eating should be flexible – it's about 'aiming' for balance rather than sticking to strict rules and stressing about what your eat. Even portion sizes aren't completely set in stone, so if you eat a steak slightly larger than the standard portion size for lunch, just have a smaller protein portion at dinner. As long as it all adds up at the end of the day (or comes pretty close) you can go to bed feeling confident that you've moved another step closer towards your weight-loss goals.

FLAVOUR BOOSTERS
Add a sprinkle of herbs and spices to make your meals even tastier (plus you won't need to use as much salt). Nuts and seeds – such as sesame, sunflower and pepitas (pumpkin kernels) – are also good for extra flavour and crunch.

FATS AND OILS
Drizzle a healthy oil (see p15) over your vegetables or use in a simple salad dressing. Adding nuts, seeds and avocado is another way to enjoy healthy fats.

½ serve of grains

YOUR DAILY SERVES CAN BE SPREAD ACROSS THE WHOLE DAY IN ANY WAY THAT WORKS FOR YOU.

BREAKFAST
CHERRY & YOGHURT MUESLI CUPS,
see recipe p 48.

½ serve of dairy

1 serve of fruit

1½ serves of vegies

LUNCH
ROAST BEEF & CARAMELISED ONION ROLL,
see recipe p57.

½ serve of lean meat

1 serve of grains

2½ serves of vegies

1 serve of lean meat

DINNER
MUSTARD & BROWN SUGAR PORK WITH COLESLAW,
see recipe p90.

½ serve of vegies & ¼ serve of fruit

Good health quiz

Take our quick quiz and discover some new healthy habits that will benefit your weight loss and your general health. Circle the numbers next to your answers (1, 2 or 3), then add these up for your grand total. The closer your score is to 60, the less changes you need to make.

1. Do you eat fruit every day?
1   More than five pieces.
2   Less than two pieces.
3   Two pieces.

Make a healthy swap and eat at least two serves of fruit a day to get a variety of unique nutrients. Fruit is a **Filling & Healthy Food**, so it will fill you up for relatively few kilojoules.

2. How many serves of vegetables do you eat a day?
1   None.
2   Three servings or less.
3   Five servings or more.

Eat at least five serves of vegetables a day. Vegetables are **Filling & Healthy Foods**, so they will fill you up for relatively few kilojoules.

3. What sort of bread do you choose to eat most often?
1   White bread.
2   Wholemeal bread.
3   Wholegrain, multigrain, soy and linseed, rye or oat bread.

Choose wholegrains wherever possible. Wholegrains provide more vitamins, minerals and fibre, plus greater satisfaction than white bread.

4. Which type of pasta and rice do you usually eat?
1   Don't eat pasta or rice.
2   White pasta and white rice.
3   Wholemeal pasta and brown rice whenever I can.

Choose wholemeal pasta or brown rice for extra vitamins, minerals and fibre and greater satisfaction.

5. Do you trim fat from meat and remove skin from chicken?
1   Never.
2   Sometimes.
3   Always.

Reducing the amount of saturated fat in your diet helps lower the risk of high cholesterol and is good for heart health. Choose lean meat and trim any fat or skin.

6. Do you take a multivitamin each day?
1   Never.
2   Most days.
3   Every day.

Get the necessary nutrients for healthy weight loss by following the recommendations of our Good Health Guidelines, which includes a daily multivitamin.

7. How often do you eat nuts and seeds?
1   Never.
2   Sometimes.
3   Every day.

Add portion-controlled healthy fats such as nuts and seed to your salads, meals and snacks. Not only do they provide a delicious crunch, they can also help lower cholesterol.

8. How many glasses of fluids do you drink in a day?
1   Less than three (< 0.75L).
3   Three to five (0.75L–1.25L).
3   Six to eight (1.5L–2L).

Try to drink at least 1.5L–2L fluid each day. Water, tea, coffee, broth (clear soup), reduced-fat milk, juice and diet soft drinks all count towards the total.

9. Do you add salt to your cooking and food?
1   Usually.
2   Sometimes.
3   Rarely.

Choose foods that are low in salt. Try using fresh herbs and lemon juice to add flavour instead of salt.

10. *Do you include Filling & Healthy Foods (see p9) in each of your meals?*

1 Rarely/never.
2 Occasionally.
3 At every meal and sometimes for snacks.

Choose **Filling & Healthy Foods** wherever you can to help you stay satisfied and give your body the nutrients it needs.

11. *How often do you drink soft drinks and eat sugary foods such as biscuits and cakes?*

1 Every day.
2 Most days.
3 Occasionally or never.

It's best to eat only moderate amounts of sugar and foods containing processed sugar. Try mineral water with a squeeze of lime juice or naturally sweet fruit such as fresh dates.

12. *What oils or dressings do you use on salads and in cooking?*

1 Mayonnaise or creamy dressings.
2 Sesame, walnut, pumpkin or peanut oils.
3 Olive, safflower, sunflower, linseed/flaxseed or canola oils.

For a healthy swap, replace your usual oil with olive, safflower, sunflower, linseed/flaxseed or canola oils and use reduced-fat or fat-free mayonnaise or dressings.

13. *Do you eat oily fish?*

1 Never.
2 Once a week.
3 Twice a week or more.

Try to include oily fish such as salmon, mackerel and tuna in meals at least twice a week. High in beneficial omega-3 fatty acids, oily fish may help protect against heart disease.

14. *Do you eat dairy products?*

1 Never.
2 One serve a day.
3 Two to four serves a day.

Eat at least two serves of dairy products each day. Reduced or low-fat varieties are actually higher in calcium than those using whole milk.

15. *How much alcohol do you drink?*

1 More than two standard* drinks daily.
2 Two standard drinks daily.
3 No more than two standard drinks daily with one or two alcohol-free days each week.

Moderate alcohol consumption for men and women is no more than two standard drinks per day and no more than four standard drinks on any one occasion. Plan to have one or two alcohol-free days each week. * The volume of a standard drink depends on the type of alcohol consumed. Visit www.nhmrc.gov.au/your-health/alcohol-guidelines for more information.

16. *Do you include wholegrain breakfast cereals in your diet?*

1 Never.
2 Sometimes.
3 Every day.

Choose wholegrain cereals such as wheat biscuits and rolled oats for extra protein, fibre and greater satisfaction.

17. *How often do you eat fried food?*

1 Daily.
2 Two to three times a week.
3 Less than once a week.

Use cooking methods such as steaming, poaching, grilling, roasting and stewing whenever you can. When you fry foods, use a non-stick pan and an oil spray, or apply oil to the pan or food with a silicone brush.

18. *Do you eat beans and lentils (legumes)?*

1 Rarely/never.
2 Sometimes.
3 Weekly.

Add legumes such as beans, lentils and chickpeas to meals. They're rich in protein, fibre, vitamins, minerals and phytonutrients, but contain little or no fat.

19. *How often do you eat takeaway food?*

1 Daily.
2 Once or twice a week.
3 Occasionally.

Make a healthy swap and choose home-cooked meals wherever you can. If choosing takeaway food, look for those containing **Filling & Healthy Foods** and prepared using healthier cooking methods.

20. *Is the portion size of your meat, fish or poultry equal to the size of your palm?*

1 Never.
2 Sometimes.
3 Always.

Include one to two serves of lean protein each day. Use the palm of your hand as a guide to the correct portion size for cooked meat, fish or chicken.

Quick & easy meal planning

SPEND A FEW MINUTES PLANNING YOUR MEALS AND YOU'LL SAVE TIME, MONEY AND ALWAYS HAVE SOMETHING TASTY FOR YOUR TABLE.

Planning your meals in advance has many benefits as it can:

- save time (shopping is quicker and cooking is too)
- save money (you only spend money on the food you need)
- reduce waste (less food ends up in the bin)
- reduce stress (no more 'what's for dinner?' panic attacks).

When it comes to weight loss, meal planning has another great advantage. If you figure out your meals and any snacks in advance you are less likely to be tempted by unhealthier quick-fix options. Planning also helps you to eat regularly and listen to your hunger signals. If you wait until you are ravenous, you are more likely to overeat.

Another benefit of planning your meals is that it makes it easier to get the balance right (see p12). Be sure to include plenty of **Filling & Healthy Foods** (see p9) and choose foods that you really enjoy.

When planning, think about how much time you have to prepare your meals. Take into account busy days when you'll need a quick stir-fry and less hectic days when you have time to cook something 'slow'. You can plan for the week ahead, a few days in advance or just a day at a time — it's completely up to you. See our tasty meal ideas (p26) to see how it's done.

A new way to plan your day

At Weight Watchers, we love tracking. That's because it lets us enjoy a wide variety of foods and gives an insight into our eating habits. But it's not the only way to lose weight. Weight Watchers **Filling & Healthy Foods** provide another way. These foods are so satisfying that it's possible to lose weight simply by focusing mostly on them. We call this a Filling & Healthy Day.

What is a Filling & Healthy Day?

On a Filling & Healthy Day you focus on eating **Filling & Healthy Foods** without counting their *ProPoints* values or portion sizes. Instead, use your levels of satisfaction as your guide to how much to eat.

It works because **Filling & Healthy Foods** are often great sources of protein, or they're packed with water or fibre. These elements create a lasting sensation of fullness, so you're likely to eat less over the course of a day. **Filling & Healthy Foods** are also lower in kilojoules and have less sugar, sodium, fat (both total and saturated), plus more fibre, so they're good choices to make, even if you're not scrupulously watching your food intake.

"A Filling & Healthy Day is great for busy days when you don't have time for tracking *ProPoints*."

LUCY KELLY, SENIOR FOOD EDITOR

How to do it

- Choose a Filling & Healthy Day as often or a little as you like. Simply decide which approach to counting you want to take on a day-by-day basis.
- Focus on eating **Filling & Healthy Foods** throughout the day and eat only what you need to feel satisfied.
- Use your weekly allowance for any non-**Filling & Healthy Foods** you eat.
- Include two teaspoons of healthy oil in your meals for the day (sunflower, olive, flaxseed/linseed, canola or safflower) without counting them. This is for your good health.
- If you eat more than two teaspoons of healthy oil during the day, deduct the additional *ProPoints* values from your weekly allowance.
- There are certain drinks, seasonings and condiments you can include, too. These are listed on p42 of your *Pocket Guide*.

Monday: Plan meals (remember to check out recipes in my new cookbook!)

Tuesday: Grocery shopping – buy extra fruit & vegies for snacks.

Wednesday: Yoga class 6pm.

Thursday: Try new lamb recipe on p101.

Friday: Drinks after work.

Saturday: Family lunch at Mum's.

Sunday: Cook ahead for the week (Lasagne on p105 is good to freeze).

TRY OUR TASTY MEAL IDEAS

To help get you started, we've created some delicious seasonal meal ideas for breakfast, lunch and dinner. How you use them is entirely up to you – mix and match to suit your tastes, or simply use them as examples when creating your own meals. These meal ideas have been designed to follow our Good Health Guidelines and add up to 26 *ProPoints* values (see My Personal Daily *ProPoints* Allowance, p30, if your daily allowance is higher). But you can mix and match them however you like – just ensure you keep an eye on the *ProPoints* values (see Plan Your Day, p28) and eating is easy!

Summer meal ideas

Breakfast

 MANGO SMOOTHIE
▲ 1 cup skim milk, blended with
▲ 2 tbs low-fat natural yoghurt,
▲ 1 small mango and 2 tsp ground linseeds.

Serve with 1 slice wholegrain toast, spread with 2 tsp honey.

 CEREAL & FRUIT
▲ 2 whole-wheat biscuits, topped with
▲ 1 peach (sliced), ▲ ½ cup skim milk and 2 tsp ground linseeds.

Serve with 1 skim-milk coffee.

Lunch

8 NIÇOISE SALAD
▲ 1 cup lettuce, tossed with ▲ 1 medium potato (steamed, cooled, diced),
▲ 1 boiled egg (sliced), ▲ ½ cup green beans (sliced), 95g can tuna in brine (drained), ▲ 5 cherry tomatoes (halved), 6 kalamata olives in brine, 1 tsp balsamic vinegar and 1 tsp flaxseed oil.

Finish with 2 fresh dates.

7 CHILLI CHICKEN WRAP
See page 71 for recipe.

Dinner

9 MUSTARD & BROWN SUGAR PORK WITH COLESLAW
See page 90 for recipe.

8 LEMON SQUID WITH MEDITERRANEAN SALAD
See page 107 for recipe.

1 Finish with ▲ 3 tbs low-fat natural yoghurt with ▲ ½ cup berries.

Snacks

3 1 small skim-milk coffee.
1 tbs mashed avocado with
0 *ProPoints* value vegie sticks
(▲ cucumber, ▲ carrot, ▲ celery,
▲ capsicum).
▲ 1 peach.
▲ 1 cup cherries.

4 ▲ ½ cup skim milk for tea/coffee.
▲ 1 nectarine.
▲ 1 Ryvita multigrain crispbread topped with 30g smoked salmon.
▲ 150g tub NESTLÉ SOLEIL DIET Yoghurt.

Meal ideas designed for a daily allowance of 26 *ProPoints* values.

7 **SOURDOUGH WITH PEANUT BUTTER & BANANA BERRY SALAD**
See page 43 for recipe.

3 **FRUIT SALAD WITH SPICED PISTACHIO YOGHURT**
See page 40 for recipe.

6 **BIRCHER MUESLI**
▲ ½ cup rolled oats, combined with ▲ ½ apple (grated), ½ tsp ground cinnamon, ¼ cup water and ¼ cup orange juice. Soak overnight. Add ▲ 2 tbs low-fat natural yoghurt just before serving. Top with 5 almonds.

6 **BEEF & WHITE BEAN SALAD**
▲ 1 cup baby spinach, tossed with ▲ ½ cup canned white beans (rinsed, drained), ▲ ½ carrot (sliced), ▲ 2 slices (88g) deli-sliced roast beef, 1 tbs chopped parsley, 1 tsp capers, 2 tsp lemon juice and 1 tsp olive oil.

5 **TURKEY ROLL**
1 medium wholegrain roll, spread with 1 tbs hommus and filled with 50g deli-sliced lean turkey breast, ▲ ½ carrot (grated) and ▲ ⅓ cup baby spinach leaves.

Finish with ▲ 1 cup fresh fruit salad.

6 **FAST CAESAR SALAD**
See page 54 for recipe.

6 **SWEET POTATO, RED ONION & FETA FRITTATA**
See page 81 for recipe. Serve with suggested side salad.

4 Finish with 1 Weight Watchers Cheesecake Passionfruit Burst.

10 **SOBA NOODLE & TUNA SALAD**
See page 69 for recipe.

3 Enjoy with 150ml glass McWilliam's Balance Semillon Sauvignon Blanc.

9 **ZUCCHINI, CORN & HALOUMI FRITTERS**
See page 70 for recipe. Serve with suggested side salad, drizzled with 1 tsp flaxseed oil.

Finish with ▲ 1 cup chopped rockmelon.

3 1 small skim-milk cappuccino.
0 *ProPoints* value vegie sticks (▲ carrot, ▲ celery, ▲ cucumber) with 1 tbs tomato salsa.
1 cup green tea.
▲ 1 cup grapes topped with ▲ 3 tbs low-fat natural yoghurt.

5 ▲ ½ cup skim milk for tea/coffee.
▲ 1 fresh apricot.
▲ 1 cup salad leaves, tossed with 1 tsp balsamic vinegar, 1 tsp flaxseed oil and 30g smoked salmon.
1 Mango & lime smoothie – see page 137 for recipe.

5 1 small skim-milk cappuccino.
▲ ½ punnet strawberries.
▲ ½ cup chopped fresh pineapple.
▲ 150g tub NESTLÉ SOLEIL DIET Yoghurt.
10 wholegrain rice crackers with ▲ 1 tbs Weight Watchers Cottage Cheese.

Autumn meal ideas

Plan your day

If you choose one of the higher *ProPoints* value breakfast, lunch, dinner or snack options when mixing and matching these meal ideas, choose lower *ProPoints* value options for the rest of the day to stay within your daily *ProPoints* allowance (see My Personal Daily *ProPoints* Allowance, p30, if your daily allowance is higher than 26). Alternatively, use some *ProPoints* values from your weekly budget or your exercise bonus points to make up the shortfall.

Why seasonal ideas?

Two main reasons – convenience and taste. We've used lots of **Filling & Healthy Foods** in our meal ideas, which means lots of fruit and vegies. We've then focused on what's in season, so ingredients are easier to find at the shops and often much cheaper, too.

Also, seasonal produce is picked then delivered straight to the store, with very little time in cold storage. This makes it much tastier (so you'll enjoy it even more) and means you're eating fruit and vegies at their nutritional peak (some nutrients are lost during long periods in cold storage). Seasonal eating is also about matching meals with the type of food you want to eat at certain times of the year – a fresh salad is always great in summer, while winter is the time for cooked breakfasts and warming soups.

Breakfast

7 PAN-FRIED MUSHROOMS ON WHOLEGRAIN TOAST
See page 38 for recipe.

6 CEREAL WITH ALMONDS & FIGS
▲ 2 whole-wheat biscuits, topped with ▲ ½ cup skim milk, ▲ 2 fresh figs (sliced) and 10 raw almonds.

Lunch

5 PUY LENTIL SOUP
See page 58 for recipe.

5 CHEESE & TOMATO TOASTED SANDWICH
2 slices multigrain bread, filled with ▲ 1 tomato (sliced) and 1 slice Bega So Extra Light 50% tasty cheese. Cook in sandwich press until toasted.

Dinner

7 STEAK WITH EGGPLANT RELISH & ROAST POTATOES
See page 102 for recipe. Serve with suggested side vegetables.

3 Finish with 1 tub Weight Watchers Cookies and Cream Ice Cream.

10 PIRI PIRI CHICKEN WITH WARM COUSCOUS SALAD
See page 85 for recipe. Serve with suggested side salad.

Snacks

4 1 small skim-milk cappuccino.
▲ 1 plum.
▲ 1 nashi.
▲ 150g tub NESTLÉ SOLEIL DIET Yoghurt, topped with ▲ ½ cup grapes.
1 Bacon & corn polenta muffin – see page 134 for recipe.

5 ▲ ½ cup skim milk for tea/coffee.
▲ 1 kiwifruit.
▲ 1 passionfruit.
▲ 1 cup air-popped popcorn.
Banana smoothie: Blend ▲ 1 cup skim milk with ▲ 2 tbs low-fat natural yoghurt and ▲ 1 small banana.
0 *ProPoints* value vegie soup – see page 148 for recipe.

Meal ideas designed for a daily allowance of 26 *ProPoints* values.

5 BAKED BEANS ON TOAST

1 slice wholegrain toast, topped with 130g can Weight Watchers Baked Beans. Serve with ▲ ½ grilled tomato.

5 CEREAL WITH FRUIT

45g Weight Watchers Fruit & Fibre Tropical Cereal, topped with ▲ ½ cup skim milk and ▲ 1 small apple (sliced).

8 EGG MUFFIN

2 toasted wholegrain English muffin halves, spread with 1 tbs mashed avocado, topped with ▲ 1 boiled egg (sliced) and 30g sliced lean ham.

9 CHICKPEA, TUNA & FETA SALAD

▲ 1 cup baby spinach leaves, tossed with ▲ ½ cup canned chickpeas (rinsed, drained), ▲ ½ carrot (sliced), ▲ ¼ cucumber (sliced), ▲ ¼ red capsicum (sliced), ▲ 95g can tuna in springwater (drained), 30g reduced-fat feta cheese, 1 tsp balsamic vinegar and 1 tsp olive oil.

Finish with ▲ 150g tub NESTLÉ SOLEIL DIET Yoghurt and 2 fresh dates.

7 CHICKEN BLT

See page 63 for recipe.

7 SMOKED SALMON & FENNEL SALAD ON RYE

See page 59 for recipe. Serve with 0 *ProPoints* value ▲ baby spinach leaves.

8 ROSEMARY LAMB CUTLETS WITH CARROT ROSTI

See page 101 for recipe. Serve with suggested side vegetables.

7 OVEN-STEAMED FISH WITH ASIAN DRESSING

See page 91 for recipe.

3

Enjoy with 150ml glass McWilliam's Balance Semillon Sauvignon Blanc.

5 GINGER POACHED TOFU WITH UDON NOODLES

See page 88 for recipe.

2

Finish with ▲ 4 tbs low-fat natural yoghurt, topped with ▲ ½ punnet strawberries.

4

1 small skim-milk cappuccino.
▲ 1 orange.
▲ 1 plum.
▲ 1 Ryvita multigrain crispbread topped with ▲ ½ tomato (sliced).
0 *ProPoints* value vegie sticks (▲ carrot, ▲ celery, ▲ capsicum) with 2 tbs tomato salsa.
1 Oat biscuit – see page 139 for recipe.

4

▲ ½ cup skim milk for tea/coffee.
▲ 150g tub NESTLÉ SOLEIL DIET Yoghurt.
▲ ½ cup grapes.
▲ 1 pear.
▲ 1 Ryvita multigrain crispbread, topped with 1 slice Bega So Extra Light 50% tasty cheese and ▲ sliced cucumber.

4

1 small skim-milk cappuccino.
0 *ProPoints* value vegie soup – see page 148 for recipe.
▲ 1 banana.
▲ 1 mandarin.
1 Weight Watchers Caramel Profiterole.

My personal daily *ProPoints* allowance

If your personal daily *ProPoints* allowance is higher than 26 *ProPoints* values, you can easily adapt these meal ideas to suit your needs. Simply increase the portion sizes, add extra healthy foods to your meals or increase snacks and treats. Try these ideas:

1 tsp healthy oil (flaxseed oil, olive oil etc).
1 tsp Weight Watchers Canola Spread.
1 tbs hommus.

1 egg.
95g can tuna in springwater.
1 small skim-milk coffee.
10 rice crackers.
1 Weight Watchers Choc Crisp bar.
1 packet Weight Watchers Nibblies.
1 medium potato.

1 medium (50g) wholegrain bread roll.
150g tub low-fat natural yoghurt.
1 corn on the cob.
½ cup baked beans.
100g grilled lean chicken breast.
1 Weight Watchers Fruit Cereal Bar.

1 tbs peanut butter.
1 Weight Watchers Cereal Nut Bar.
30g dried fruit and nut mix.

1 cup cooked pasta.

Winter meal ideas

Breakfast

5 SPICED FRUIT PORRIDGE
See page 49 for recipe.

9 BREAKFAST WRAP WITH PESTO SCRAMBLED EGGS
See page 46 for recipe.

Lunch

6 BEEF & SALAD SANDWICH
2 slices multigrain bread, spread with 1 tbs mashed avocado and filled with
▲ 50g thinly sliced rare roast beef,
▲ ½ tomato (sliced), ▲ ½ carrot (grated), ▲ ½ cup mixed salad leaves.

2 Finish with 1 Weight Watchers Choc Crisp Original bar.

6 CHICKEN, PUMPKIN & BEAN SOUP
See page 72 for recipe.

Dinner

9 SOUTHERN BAKED CHICKEN WITH CORN
See page 87 for recipe. Serve with suggested side vegetable, drizzled with 1 tsp flaxseed oil.

Finish with 1 cup peppermint tea.

10 DOUBLE-DUTY LASAGNE
See page 105 for recipe. Serve with suggested side salad.

Snacks

4 1 small skim-milk cappuccino.
▲ 1 banana.
▲ 1 pear.
▲ 150g tub NESTLÉ SOLEIL DIET Yoghurt.
1 Wholemeal pikelet – see page 142 for recipe.

1 ▲ ½ cup skim milk for tea/coffee.
▲ 1 apple.
▲ 1 mandarin.
▲ ½ punnet strawberries.
1 bowl Tomato & carrot soup – see page 145 for recipe.

Meal ideas designed for a daily allowance of 26 *ProPoints* values.

7 CHERRY & YOGHURT MUESLI CUPS
See page 48 for recipe.

4 VEGEMITE MUFFIN
2 toasted multigrain English muffin halves, spread with 1 tbs low-fat smooth ricotta cheese and 2 tsp Vegemite. Top with ▲ ½ tomato (sliced).

5 PEAR CEREAL
½ cup Weight Watchers Fruit & Fibre Tropical Cereal, with ▲ ½ cup skim milk and ▲ 1 small pear (sliced).

Serve with 1 small skim-milk cappuccino.

7 ROAST BEEF & CARAMELISED ONION ROLL
See page 57 for recipe.

7 JACKET POTATO
▲ 1 medium baked potato, topped with ▲ ¼ red onion (finely chopped), ▲ ¼ cup corn kernels (drained), ▲ ½ tomato (chopped), 1 tbs extra-light sour cream, ▲ ½ cup baby spinach leaves and 30g Bega So Extra Light 50% grated cheese.

9 CHICKEN & CHEESE MELT
2 toasted multigrain English muffin halves, topped with ▲ 50g cooked skinless lean chicken breast, ▲ 1 tomato (sliced) and 2 tbs Bega So Extra Light 50% grated cheese. Grill until melted. Serve with ▲ 1 cup mixed salad leaves, ▲ ½ cucumber (chopped) and ▲ ¼ red capsicum (chopped), tossed with 1 tsp balsamic vinegar and 1 tsp flaxseed oil.

8 SEAFOOD HOT-POT
See page 108 for recipe.

10 SPAGHETTI WITH FRESH TOMATO SAUCE & BOCCONCINI
See page 100 for recipe. Serve with suggested side.

2 Finish with 1 Weight Watchers Belgian Eclair.

10 BARBECUED SUMAC LAMB WITH FATTOUSH & BABA GANOUSH
See page 78 for recipe.

4 1 small skim-milk cappuccino.
▲ 1 passionfruit.
1 cup miso soup.
▲ 1 nashi.
▲ 1 kiwifruit.
1 cup steamed 0 *ProPoints* value
▲ vegetables, drizzled with 1 tsp flaxseed oil.

3 1 small skim-milk cappuccino.
2 dried figs.
1 bowl 0 *ProPoints* value vegie soup – see p148 for recipe.
▲ 1 orange.
2 fresh dates.

2 ▲ 1 cup fresh fruit salad.
▲ 150g tub NESTLÉ SOLEIL DIET Yoghurt.
▲ 1 Ryvita multigrain crispbread topped with 1 tbs low-fat smooth ricotta cheese and 1 small banana (sliced).
▲ ½ punnet cherry tomatoes.
▲ 1 apple.

Spring meal ideas

My weekly *ProPoints* allowance

How you spend your optional weekly *ProPoints* allowance of 49 is entirely up to you. Some weeks you could use it to add to your daily *ProPoints* allowance, while other weeks you could use it eating out or save it up for a big event. Here are some ideas:

 1

1 tbs Weight Watchers Sour Cream.

 2

10 cashews.
1 Lindt ball.

 3

1 nip Baileys Original Irish Cream.
1 Californian sushi roll.

 4

1 Cosmopolitan cocktail.
2 Weight Watchers Lamington Fingers.

 5

150ml glass red wine.
1 cinnamon donut.

 6

375ml bottle beer.
1 slice (87g) ham and pineapple pizza.

 7

½ cup toasted muesli.

 8

1 medium (142g) salmon fillet.
1 plain croissant.

Breakfast

 6 MIXED BERRY SMOOTHIE
▲ 1 cup skim milk, blended with 2 tbs low-fat vanilla yoghurt and ▲ 1 cup fresh or frozen mixed berries.

Serve with 1 toasted wholemeal crumpet, spread with 1 tsp honey.

7 BANANA ON FRUIT TOAST
2 slices wholemeal fruit toast, spread with 2 tbs low-fat smooth ricotta cheese, topped with ▲ sliced banana.

Serve with 1 small skim-milk cappuccino.

Lunch

 8 CHICKEN & SALAD SANDWICH
2 slices wholegrain bread, filled with ▲ 100g barbecued chicken breast (skin removed), ▲ ¼ cup grated carrot, ▲ ½ tomato (sliced), ▲ ¼ small red onion (finely chopped) and ▲ ½ cup salad leaves.

 8 BROWN RICE SALAD
▲ ¾ cup cooked brown rice, mixed with 2 slices smoked salmon (chopped), ▲ ¼ red capsicum (sliced), ▲ ¼ cup sliced green beans, ▲ ½ celery stick (sliced), ▲ ½ carrot (sliced), 1 tsp salt-reduced soy sauce, 1 tsp lime juice and 1 tsp flaxseed oil.

Finish with ▲ 1 apple.

Dinner

 11 MIDDLE EASTERN BEEF MEATBALLS
See page 113 for recipe.

 10 TUSCAN PORK FILLET WITH CABBAGE SALAD
See page 94 for recipe.

Snacks

 1 ▲ ½ cup skim milk for tea/coffee.
▲ 1 apple.
▲ ½ cup sliced melon.
▲ 1 celery stick with ▲ 1 tbs Weight Watchers Cottage Cheese.

 1 ▲ 1 cup fresh fruit salad.
▲ 150g tub NESTLÉ SOLEIL DIET Yoghurt.
▲ 1 mandarin.
0 *ProPoints* value vegie sticks (▲ carrot, ▲ celery, ▲ capsicum) with 1 tbs tomato salsa.

Meal ideas designed for a daily allowance of 26 *ProPoints* values.

7 | BREAKFAST BRUSCHETTA

40g slice sourdough toast, topped with ¼ small avocado (sliced), 3 sun-dried tomatoes (not in oil), 30g reduced-fat feta cheese (crumbled) and fresh basil leaves.

8 | DATE & NUT PORRIDGE

▲ ⅓ cup traditional oats, cooked with ▲ ⅔ cup skim milk and 2 fresh dates (chopped), sprinkled with 3 raw walnuts (chopped).

Serve with 1 small skim-milk cappuccino.

7 | EGG, ASPARAGUS & SMOKED SALMON MUFFINS

See page 41 for recipe.

8 | TUNA PASTA SALAD

▲ 1 cup cooked wholemeal pasta, tossed with ▲ ½ cucumber (grated), ▲ ½ carrot (grated), ▲ 1 cup baby spinach leaves, ▲ 95g can Weight Watchers Tuna in Springwater, 1 tsp flaxseed oil and 1 tsp lemon juice. Season with salt and pepper.

Finish with ▲ 1 cup grapes.

6 | BEEF TOASTIE & SALAD

2 slices wholegrain bread, filled with ▲ 2 slices deli-sliced roast beef, ▲ 1 tomato (sliced) and 1 slice Bega So Extra Light 50% natural cheese. Cook in sandwich press until melted. Serve with ▲ 1 cup mixed salad leaves, tossed with 1 tsp balsamic vinegar and 1 tsp flaxseed oil.

5 | EGG & SALAD WRAP

I piece rye mountain bread, spread with 1 tbs avocado and topped with ▲ 1 boiled egg (sliced), 2 slices canned beetroot, ▲ ½ cup grated carrot and ▲ ½ cup salad leaves. Roll to enclose.

9 | RICOTTA & LEMON THYME-STUFFED CHICKEN

See page 93 for recipe. Serve with suggested side vegetables.

7 | CHARGRILLED VEGETABLES WITH RICOTTA & FENNEL SALT

See page 99 for recipe.

3 Serve with ▲ ½ cup steamed brown rice.

8 | STIR-FRIED SCALLOPS WITH ASIAN GREENS

See page 106 for recipe.

2 ▲ ½ cup skim milk for tea/coffee.
▲ ½ punnet strawberries.
▲ 1 Ryvita multigrain crispbread topped with ▲ 1 tbs Weight Watchers Cottage Cheese, ▲ sliced tomato and ▲ cucumber.
▲ 1 apple.

2 ▲ ½ cup skim milk for tea/coffee.
▲ 1 small mango.
▲ ½ cup pineapple.
5 wholegrain rice crackers with tomato salsa.
1 bowl 0 *ProPoints* value vegie soup – see page 148 for recipe.

6 1 skim-milk cappuccino.
▲ 1 orange.
▲ 150g tub NESTLÉ SOLEIL DIET Yoghurt.
▲ ½ papaya.
▲ 1 passionfruit.
▲ 1 cup mixed salad leaves, tossed with balsamic vinegar, 1 tsp flaxseed oil and 15g reduced-fat feta cheese (crumbled).
▲ 1 cup air-popped popcorn.

Recipes

As we've shown, it's easy to create your own delicious and balanced meals. But on those days when you need a bit of inspiration or want to try something new, our recipes are just the thing. We've worked out all the **ProPoints** values and portion sizes for you, so the only thing you need to do is write a shopping list and get cooking.

Our recipes not only provide 'the complete meal' but a complete day's worth of meals! We've covered everything from satisfying breakfasts and lunches to delicious dinners and desserts, with some tasty snack ideas in between. Cooking these recipes is a great way to become familiar with what standard portion sizes for weight loss look like and how to achieve balance on your plate.

There is something for everyone – from traditional favourites such as Lasagne (p105) and Apple strudel (p127) to fresh new ideas using exotic flavours, such as Middle Eastern meatballs (p113) and Orange blossom panna cotta (p122). All our ingredients are widely available and our easy-to-follow instructions make them simple for anyone to cook.

We've also marked all our **Filling & Healthy Foods** with a green triangle ▲ and taste-tested each recipe to make sure it's delicious and satisfying. So all you have to do is flick through the pages and decide what to cook for your next mouth-watering meal. Enjoy!

LUCY KELLY
Senior Food Editor,
Weight Watchers member since 1996

5 QUICK BREAKFAST IDEAS

1 CLASSIC PORRIDGE: 40g traditional rolled oats, cooked with ¾ cup (185ml) cold water and ¼ tsp salt (optional). Serve sprinkled with 2 tsp brown sugar and 2 tbs skim milk or equivalent.

2 SMOKED SALMON, EGG & TOMATO: 1 slice wholegrain toast, topped with 1 egg (poached, fried with oil spray, or soft boiled), 30g sliced smoked salmon and 1 medium tomato (grilled).

3 FRUIT SALAD & YOGHURT: 1 cup diced fruit salad (such as apple, orange, banana, passionfruit, pear and kiwifruit), topped with 100g low-fat honey yoghurt and 3 walnuts (chopped).

4 FRUIT & MUESLI: ½ cup (55g) natural muesli (with nuts, seeds and dried fruit), topped with ¼ cup (60ml) skim milk and ½ cup chopped fresh fruit.

5 BREKKIE WRAP: 1 wholegrain wrap, spread with 1 tbs mashed avocado and filled with 1 egg (scrambled), 1 medium tomato (chopped) and 2 teaspoons barbecue sauce.

5 *ProPoints* VALUES PER SERVE | SERVES: 1

5 *ProPoints* VALUES PER SERVE | SERVES: 1

5 *ProPoints* VALUES PER SERVE | SERVES: 1

7 *ProPoints* VALUES PER SERVE | SERVES: 1

7 *ProPoints* VALUES PER SERVE | SERVES: 1

Breakfast

WHY IS BREAKFAST IMPORTANT?

When you enjoy a wholesome breakfast, you're likely to make better food choices throughout the day. Breakfast eaters are also more likely to meet the recommended dietary intakes of key nutrients than those who skip. A good brekkie combo is carbohydrates and protein – carbs provide energy to get up and go, while protein keeps you feeling fuller for longer.

GIVE YOUR TASTEBUDS A DELICIOUS
WAKE-UP CALL WITH THIS TASTY
COMBINATION OF MARINATED FETA AND
EARTHY MUSHROOMS ON TOAST.

Pan-fried mushrooms
on wholegrain toast

 7 *ProPoints* VALUES PER SERVE | SERVES: 2 | PREP: 5 MINS | COOKING TIME: 10 MINS

2 tsp olive oil
▲ **6 medium field mushrooms (see tip)**
2 x 40g slices wholegrain bread
60g marinated goat's feta cheese
1 tbs coarsely chopped fresh chives

*Filling & Healthy Foods are marked with a green triangle.
These foods help fill you up and keep you healthy.*

1 Heat oil in a large non-stick frying pan over high heat. Cook mushrooms, in batches, for 2–3 minutes each side or until golden. Season with salt and freshly ground black pepper.
2 Meanwhile, grill or toast bread on both sides until lightly browned. Serve toast topped with mushrooms, feta and chives.
NOTE: You can use any marinated feta cheese instead of goat's feta. The ***ProPoints*** values remain the same.

TIP: *To prepare mushrooms, simply wipe the tops with damp paper towel and trim the stalks.*

Fruit salad with spiced pistachio yoghurt

 ProPoints VALUES PER SERVE | SERVES: 4 | PREP: 15 MINS | COOKING TIME: 5 MINS

¼ cup (35g) pistachio kernels
▲ 1 mango, cut into 2cm pieces
▲ 300g fresh pineapple, cut into 2cm pieces
▲ 2 kiwifruit, cut into 2cm pieces
▲ 250g strawberries, halved
▲ 1 passionfruit, pulp removed
  ¼ cup shredded fresh mint leaves
▲ 2 x 150g tubs NESTLÉ SOLEIL DIET Vanilla
    Flavoured Yoghurt
  1 tbs honey
  ½ tsp ground mixed spice

Filling & Healthy Foods are marked with a green triangle.
These foods help fill you up and keep you healthy.

1 Preheat oven to 180°C or 160°C fan-forced. Spread
pistachios on a baking tray and bake for 3–5 minutes
or until toasted. Cool and chop finely.
2 Place mango, pineapple, kiwifruit, strawberries,
passionfruit and mint in a large bowl. Toss gently
to combine.
3 Mix yoghurt, honey, mixed spice and half the
pistachios in a small bowl until combined.
4 Serve fruit salad topped with spiced pistachio
yoghurt and sprinkled with remaining pistachios.

TIP: To prepare mango, use a sharp knife to cut
down either side of the stone to remove the 'cheeks'.
Cut the flesh in a diamond pattern, then push the
cheeks inside out and slice off the pieces of mango
close to the skin.

Egg, asparagus & smoked salmon muffins

 7 *ProPoints* VALUES PER SERVE | SERVES: 2 | PREP: 10 MINS | COOKING TIME: 5 MINS

▲ **2 eggs**
▲ **4 asparagus spears**
  2 tsp extra-virgin olive oil
  2 tsp lemon juice
  2 tsp finely chopped fresh dill, plus
    extra sprigs to garnish
  ¼ tsp Dijon mustard
  2 x 60g wholegrain English muffins, split
  60g sliced smoked salmon
  Lemon wedges, to serve

Filling & Healthy Foods are marked with a green triangle.
These foods help fill you up and keep you healthy.

1 Half-fill a large frying pan with water and bring to
a simmer. Carefully crack 1 egg into a small cup.
Carefully slide egg out of cup into the water. Repeat
with remaining egg. Poach eggs gently for 1–2 minutes
or until egg whites are set and yolks remain soft. Remove
eggs with a slotted spoon. Drain on a plate lined with
paper towel.
2 Meanwhile, place asparagus in a heatproof bowl and
cover with boiling water. Set aside for 1–2 minutes or
until bright green and just tender. Drain.
3 Whisk oil, juice, chopped dill and mustard in a small
bowl until combined.
4 Grill or toast muffin halves on both sides until lightly
browned. Top muffins with salmon, asparagus and eggs.
Drizzle with dill dressing and serve with a sprig of dill
and a lemon wedge.

TIP: You can use 2 slices (42g) Weight Watchers
*Bacon (grilled) instead of salmon. The **ProPoints***
values remain the same.

Sourdough with peanut butter & banana berry salad

 ProPoints VALUES PER SERVE | SERVES: 2 | PREP: 10 MINS | COOKING TIME: 5 MINS

▲ **1 banana, sliced**
▲ **100g strawberries, sliced**
▲ **⅓ cup (55g) raspberries**
▲ **¼ cup (45g) blueberries**
  2 tsp honey (see tip)
  2 x 30g slices wholemeal sourdough bread
  2 tbs peanut butter

*Filling & Healthy Foods are marked with a green triangle.
These foods help fill you up and keep you healthy.*

1 Combine banana, strawberries, raspberries and blueberries in a medium bowl and drizzle with honey. Toss gently to combine. Set aside for 5 minutes.

2 Meanwhile, grill or toast bread on both sides until lightly browned. Spread toast with peanut butter and serve topped with banana berry salad.

TIP: *Honey is easier to measure and drizzle if you warm it in a microwave-safe container on High (100%) for a few seconds. Alternatively, heat the measuring spoon in hot water first.*

ADD SOME PIZZAZZ TO PLAIN PEANUT BUTTER ON TOAST BY SERVING IT WITH A PRETTY MEDLEY OF FRESH FRUITS LIGHTLY DRIZZLED IN HONEY.

Boston beans & sausages

ProPoints VALUES PER SERVE | SERVES: 4 | PREP: 15 MINS | COOKING TIME: 20 MINS

- 8 (245g) extra-lean beef chipolata sausages (see note)
- ▲ 1 brown onion, finely chopped
- 1 garlic clove, thinly sliced
- 1 tsp mild paprika
- ½ tsp smoked paprika
- 1 tbs golden syrup (see tip)
- ▲ 400g can whole tomatoes
- ▲ 400g can four bean mix, rinsed, drained
- 4 x 30g slices multigrain bread

Filling & Healthy Foods are marked with a green triangle. These foods help fill you up and keep you healthy.

1 Lightly spray a large non-stick frying pan with oil and heat over medium heat. Add sausages and cook, turning, for 3–4 minutes or until browned. Transfer to a plate.

2 Lightly spray same pan with oil. Add onion and cook, stirring, for 5 minutes or until softened. Add garlic and paprikas and cook, stirring, for 30 seconds. Add syrup and cook, stirring, for 30 seconds.

3 Return sausages to pan with tomatoes and beans and bring to the boil. Reduce heat to low and simmer for 8–10 minutes or until sauce has thickened.

4 Meanwhile, grill or toast bread on both sides until lightly browned. Serve toast topped with Boston beans and sausages.

NOTE: We used Peppercorn brand chipolata sausages. You can use any extra-lean sausages (halved if large) instead of chipolatas. The **ProPoints** values remain the same.

*TIP: You can use molasses instead of golden syrup for a richer sauce. The **ProPoints** values remain the same.*

Buckwheat pancakes with honeyed ricotta

ProPoints VALUES PER SERVE | SERVES: 4 | PREP: 15 MINS | COOKING TIME: 10 MINS

½ cup (100g) buckwheat flour (see note)
⅓ cup (50g) wholemeal self-raising flour
½ tsp baking powder
½ tsp ground cinnamon
1 tbs sugar
▲ 1 egg
▲ 1 cup (250ml) skim milk
½ cup (120g) reduced-fat fresh ricotta cheese
2 tsp honey
▲ 200g fresh mixed berries

Filling & Healthy Foods are marked with a green triangle.
These foods help fill you up and keep you healthy.

1 Sift buckwheat and self-raising flours, baking powder and cinnamon into a medium bowl. Stir in sugar. Place egg and milk in a jug and beat with a fork until combined. Make a well in the centre of flour mixture and pour in egg mixture. Whisk until smooth. Set aside for 10 minutes.

2 Meanwhile, mix ricotta and honey in a small bowl until combined.

3 Lightly spray a large non-stick frying pan with oil and heat over medium heat. Spoon ¼ cup (60ml) batter into pan. Cook for 1–2 minutes or until bubbles rise to the surface. Turn and cook for a further 1–2 minutes or until pancake is golden. Transfer to a plate. Cover to keep warm. Repeat with remaining batter to make 8 pancakes (you can cook 2–3 at once to save time).

4 Serve pancakes topped with honeyed ricotta and berries.

NOTE: Buckwheat flour is made from crushed buckwheat seeds and has a nutty flavour. It is available in the health-food aisle of most supermarkets or from health-food stores.

Breakfast wrap with pesto scrambled eggs

 ProPoints VALUES PER SERVE | **SERVES: 2** | **PREP: 10 MINS** | **COOKING TIME: 10 MINS**

▲ **8 button mushrooms, thinly sliced**
2 tsp balsamic vinegar
▲ **2 eggs**
▲ **1 tbs skim milk**
2 tbs pesto
2 x 40g wholegrain wraps
▲ **1 tomato, finely chopped**
¼ cup (30g) Bega So Extra Light 50% grated cheese

Filling & Healthy Foods are marked with a green triangle. These foods help fill you up and keep you healthy.

1 Lightly spray a small non-stick frying pan with oil and heat over medium-high heat. Add mushrooms and cook, stirring, for 2–3 minutes or until tender and lightly browned. Stir in balsamic vinegar. Transfer to a plate. Cover to keep warm.

2 Whisk eggs and milk in a small jug until combined. Lightly spray cleaned pan with oil and heat over low heat. Pour egg mixture into pan and cook, folding occasionally (see tip), for 3–4 minutes or until cooked to your liking. Fold pesto through scrambled eggs.

3 Preheat a sandwich press. Lay wraps on a flat surface. Spoon scrambled eggs onto half of each wrap. Sprinkle with tomato, mushrooms and cheese. Fold wraps to enclose filling and cook for 2–3 minutes or until golden. Cut in half to serve.

TIP: Instead of stirring, gently fold the mixture over with a spatula as it begins to cook. This will result in light and fluffy scrambled eggs.

Cherry & yoghurt muesli cups

 ProPoints VALUES PER SERVE | **SERVES: 2** | **PREP: 15 MINS**

1 cup (200g) canned cherries in syrup
▲ 200g tub low-fat natural yoghurt
¼ cup (25g) natural muesli
2 tsp honey
5 hazelnuts, toasted, finely chopped (see note)
1 tbs pepitas (pumpkin seed kernels)

Filling & Healthy Foods are marked with a green triangle.
These foods help fill you up and keep you healthy.

1 Divide cherries and syrup among serving glasses and top with half the yoghurt. Sprinkle with muesli and top with remaining yoghurt.
2 To serve, drizzle muesli cups with honey and sprinkle with hazelnuts and pepitas.
NOTE: To toast hazelnuts, preheat oven to 180°C or 160°C fan-forced. Spread hazelnuts on a baking tray and bake for 3–5 minutes or until toasted. You can also use dry-roasted hazelnuts instead of toasting your own.

*TIP: You can use fresh pitted cherries or fresh mixed berries instead of canned cherries. The recipe will then have 5 **ProPoints** values per serve.*

Spiced fruit porridge

 ProPoints VALUES PER SERVE | SERVES: 1 | PREP: 5 MINS | COOKING TIME: 5 MINS

- ▲ ⅓ cup (30g) traditional rolled oats
  2 fresh dates, pitted, coarsely chopped
- ▲ ¼ cup (60ml) skim milk
  Pinch ground cinnamon
  Pinch ground cardamom
- ▲ 135g tub Weight Watchers Apricots, drained
  1 tsp LSA mix (see note)
  ¼ tsp brown sugar

Filling & Healthy Foods are marked with a green triangle.
These foods help fill you up and keep you healthy.

1 Place oats and dates in a small saucepan. Add milk, cinnamon, cardamom and ⅓ cup (80ml) water. Bring to the boil. Reduce heat to low and simmer, stirring, for 3–4 minutes or until cooked and thickened.
2 Serve porridge topped with apricots, LSA and brown sugar.
NOTE: LSA mix is a mixture of ground linseeds, sunflower seeds and almonds. It is available in the health-food section of most supermarkets or from health-food stores. It has a short shelf-life once opened so only buy small quantities and store it in an airtight container in the fridge.

A WARM BOWL OF PORRIDGE
LACED WITH CINNAMON,
CARDAMOM AND FRESH DATES
WILL PROVIDE A SWEET START
TO YOUR DAY.

Full-house breakfast

 ProPoints VALUES PER SERVE | SERVES: 4 | PREP: 15 MINS | COOKING TIME: 35 MINS

▲ **8 (320g) baby (chat) potatoes, halved**
▲ **250g cherry tomatoes, halved**
▲ **220g can baked beans**
   8 slices (160g) Weight Watchers Bacon
▲ **2 bunches asparagus**
▲ **4 eggs**
   4 x 30g slices wholegrain bread

Filling & Healthy Foods are marked with a green triangle.
These foods help fill you up and keep you healthy..

1 Preheat oven to 200°C or 180°C fan-forced. Line a baking tray with baking paper. Boil, steam or microwave potatoes until just tender. Drain. Place on prepared tray and spray lightly with oil. Bake for 20–25 minutes or until golden and crisp. Add tomatoes for last 10 minutes of cooking.

2 Meanwhile, place baked beans in a small saucepan over low heat. Cook, stirring, for 3–4 minutes or until heated through. Remove from heat. Cover to keep warm.

3 Lightly spray a medium non-stick frying pan with oil and heat over medium-high heat. Add bacon and cook, turning, for 4–5 minutes or until crisp and golden. Cover to keep warm. Boil, steam or microwave asparagus until just tender. Drain.

4 Half-fill a large frying pan with water and bring to a simmer. Carefully crack 1 egg into a small cup. Carefully slide egg out of cup into the water. Repeat with remaining eggs. Poach eggs gently for 1–2 minutes or until egg whites are set and yolks remain soft. Remove eggs with a slotted spoon. Drain on a plate lined with paper towel.

5 Grill or toast bread on both sides until lightly browned. Top toast with poached eggs and sprinkle with freshly ground black pepper. Serve with baked beans, bacon, asparagus and roasted potatoes and tomatoes.

*TIP: Spread toast with 1 tablespoon of Weight Watchers Canola Spread. Add 1 **ProPoints** value per serve.*

5 QUICK LUNCH IDEAS

1 **Tuna & lentil salad:** ½ cup cooked puy lentils, with ½ cup cooked brown rice, 95g can tuna in brine, I tomato, ½ celery stick, ½ Lebanese cucumber, 2 tbs low-fat cottage cheese, 2 tsp caramelised balsamic vinegar and I tsp olive oil.

2 **Chicken & chickpea salad:** 70g skinless cooked chicken breast fillet (chopped), with ½ can chickpeas, ½ cup cooked pearl barley, I cup baby rocket, ¼ red capsicum, ¼ red onion, 2 tsp currants, I tbs lemon juice, I tsp olive oil and 2 tbs fresh coriander.

3 **Roast beef wrap:** I wholegrain wrap, filled with I tbs horseradish cream, 60g sliced lean rare roast beef (fat trimmed), 2 tsp finely chopped red onion, 2 tbs finely chopped red capsicum, 3 cherry tomatoes and ½ cup chopped wild rocket.

4 **Turkey melt:** I slice wholegrain toast, topped with 30g lean roast turkey breast, 2 tsp cranberry sauce, I slice Bega So Extra Light 50% cheese. Grill until melted. Serve with I cup salad leaves, drizzled with 2 tsp balsamic vinegar and I tsp olive oil.

5 **Ham & cheese toastie with soup:** 2 slices wholegrain bread, filled with 100g 97% fat-free ham, I slice Bega So Extra Light 50% cheese and 2 tsp Dijon mustard. Cook until melted. Serve with 0 **ProPoints** value vegetable soup (see pl48).

9 **ProPoints** VALUES PER SERVE | SERVES: 1

8 **ProPoints** VALUES PER SERVE | SERVES: 1

6 **ProPoints** VALUES PER SERVE | SERVES: 1

6 **ProPoints** VALUES PER SERVE | SERVES: 1

7 **ProPoints** VALUES PER SERVE | SERVES: 1

Lunch

WHAT MAKES A GOOD LUNCH?

When you're halfway through the day you need a tasty meal that will satisfy your immediate hunger and keep you going. Try to include one serve of cooked grains, bread or starchy vegies (such as potatoes), one serve of protein, two serves of cooked vegies, salad or legumes, plus one teaspoon of healthy oil. Sitting down to enjoy it is important, too!

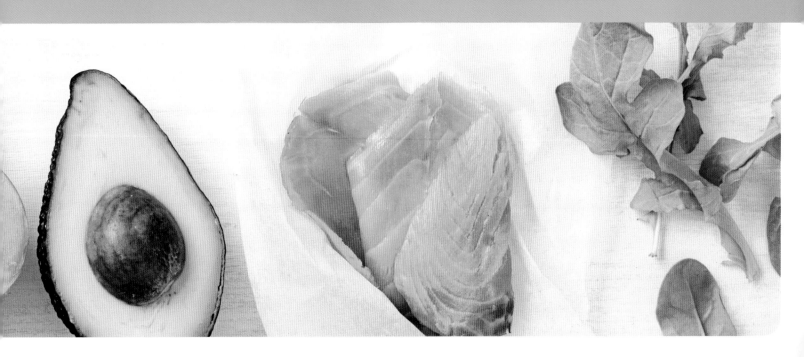

OUR TAKE ON THIS CLASSIC SALAD HAS
ALL THE GREAT FLAVOURS YOU EXPECT
BUT IS MUCH LOWER IN *ProPoints* THAN
YOUR AVERAGE CAFE-STYLE MEAL.

Fast Caesar salad

 ProPoints VALUES PER SERVE | SERVES: 4 | PREP: 15 MINS | COOKING TIME: 10 MINS

3 x 35g slices wholemeal bread
100g sliced lean prosciutto, fat trimmed
2 tbs fat-free Caesar dressing
1 tbs lemon juice
30g parmesan cheese, shaved
▲ 2 baby cos lettuce
▲ 4 soft-boiled eggs, halved (see note)

Filling & Healthy Foods are marked with a green triangle.
These foods help fill you up and keep you healthy.

1 Preheat grill to high. Lightly spray bread with oil. Grill bread for 1–2 minutes each side or until toasted. Cut into 1cm squares.
2 Grill prosciutto for 2 minutes each side or until crisp. Coarsely chop.
3 Whisk dressing and juice in a small bowl. Place croutons, prosciutto, parmesan and lettuce in a large bowl. Add dressing and toss to combine.
4 Divide salad among serving plates. Serve topped with egg and seasoned with salt and freshly ground black pepper.
NOTE: To soft-boil eggs, place room-temperature eggs in a small saucepan and cover with cold water. Bring to a boil over high heat, then reduce to a simmer and cook for 3–4 minutes.

Roast beef & caramelised onion roll

 ProPoints VALUES PER SERVE | **SERVES: 1** | **PREP: 5 MINS** | **COOKING TIME: 10 MINS**

1 tsp olive oil
▲ **½ red onion, thinly sliced**
1 x 50g wholegrain roll
1 tbs mashed avocado
▲ **½ cup (15g) green oak lettuce leaves**
▲ **1 tomato, thinly sliced**
▲ **50g sliced rare roast beef, fat trimmed**
(see note)

Filling & Healthy Foods are marked with a green triangle. These foods help fill you up and keep you healthy.

1 Heat oil in a small non-stick frying pan over low heat. Add onion and cook, stirring occasionally, for 8–10 minutes or until very soft and caramelised.
2 Cut roll in half and spread bottom half with avocado. Top with lettuce, tomato, beef and caramelised onion. Serve.
NOTE: Rare roast beef is available from the deli counter of most supermarkets.

*TIP: You can use 1 tablespoon of horseradish sauce instead of avocado. The recipe will then have 6 **ProPoints** values per serve.*

Puy lentil soup

ProPoints VALUES PER SERVE | **SERVES: 8** | **PREP: 20 MINS** | **COOKING TIME: 1 HOUR 10 MINS**

2 tbs olive oil
▲ 2 brown onions, finely chopped
▲ 4 celery sticks, thinly sliced
▲ 3 carrots, chopped
50g pancetta, fat trimmed, chopped
3 garlic cloves, crushed
▲ 6 tomatoes
▲ 1½ cups (300g) dried puy lentils (see note)
1.75L (7 cups) chicken stock
½ cup finely chopped fresh flat-leaf parsley leaves

Filling & Healthy Foods are marked with a green triangle.
These foods help fill you up and keep you healthy.

1 Heat oil in a large saucepan over medium heat. Add
onion, celery and carrot and cook, stirring occasionally,
for 10 minutes or until softened. Add pancetta and cook,
stirring, for 5 minutes or until vegetables are soft and
lightly golden. Add garlic and cook, stirring, for 1 minute.
2 Meanwhile, use a small knife to cut a small cross into
the base of each tomato. Place tomatoes in a large
heatproof bowl and pour over enough boiling water to
cover. Set aside for 5 minutes. Using tongs, lift tomatoes
from water and set aside until cool enough to handle.
Peel and discard tomato skins. Remove and discard the
cores and roughly chop the flesh.
3 Add tomatoes to onion mixture and cook for 5–7 minutes
or until softened. Add lentils and stock. Cover and bring to
the boil. Reduce heat to low and simmer for 45 minutes or
until lentils are tender. Serve sprinkled with parsley.
NOTE: Puy lentils, also known as French green lentils,
are small green-blue coloured lentils. They are available
in the soup section of most supermarkets.

TIP: This soup is suitable to freeze. Ladle cooled
soup into individual portion-sized airtight
containers, leaving a 1–2cm gap at the top for
expansion. Label, date and freeze for up to 2 months.
Thaw in the fridge overnight before reheating in
the microwave or a saucepan.

Smoked salmon & fennel salad on rye

 ProPoints VALUES PER SERVE | **SERVES: 2** | **PREP: 15 MINS** | **COOKING TIME: 5 MINS**

▲ **2 eggs**
2 tbs light cream cheese, softened
1 tbs lemon juice
1 tbs finely chopped fresh dill
▲ **1 fennel bulb, shaved (see tip)**
1 tbs finely chopped capers
2 x 35g slices rye bread
100g sliced smoked salmon
1 tbs coarsely chopped fresh flat-leaf parsley leaves

Filling & Healthy Foods are marked with a green triangle.
These foods help fill you up and keep you healthy.

1 Half-fill a large frying pan with water and bring to a simmer. Carefully crack 1 egg into a small cup. Carefully slide egg out of cup into the water. Repeat with remaining egg. Poach eggs gently for 1–2 minutes or until egg whites are set and yolks remain soft. Remove eggs using a slotted spoon. Drain on a plate lined with paper towel.
2 Meanwhile, combine cheese, juice and dill in a medium bowl. Add fennel and capers and toss to combine. Season fennel salad with freshly ground black pepper.
3 Grill or toast bread on both sides until lightly browned. Top with fennel salad, smoked salmon and poached eggs. Serve sprinkled with parsley.
SERVE WITH: 0 *ProPoints* value baby spinach leaves.

TIP: For very thin fennel slices, shave it with a mandolin or V-slicer. Both are available at kitchenware shops and department stores.

Zucchini, chickpea & semi-dried tomato pasta

 ProPoints VALUES PER SERVE | **SERVES: 4** | **PREP: 15 MINS** | **COOKING TIME: 15 MINS**

▲ **250g wholemeal penne pasta**
 2 tsp olive oil
▲ **1 red onion, finely chopped**
 2 garlic cloves, crushed
▲ **2 zucchini, thinly sliced**
 1 tsp finely grated lemon rind
 ¼ cup (60ml) lemon juice
▲ **2 x 400g cans chickpeas, rinsed, drained**
 ⅓ cup (50g) fat-free semi-dried tomatoes, coarsely chopped
 ⅓ cup (25g) finely grated parmesan cheese

Filling & Healthy Foods are marked with a green triangle. These foods help fill you up and keep you healthy.

1 Cook pasta in a large saucepan of boiling salted water, following packet instructions, or until just tender. Drain. Return to pan.

2 Meanwhile, heat oil in a large non-stick frying pan over medium heat. Add onion and cook, stirring, for 5 minutes or until softened. Add garlic and zucchini and cook, stirring, for 3 minutes or until zucchini is just tender. Add rind, juice, chickpeas and tomatoes and stir until hot.

3 Add zucchini mixture to pasta. Season with salt and freshly ground black pepper. Serve hot or cold sprinkled with parmesan.

SERVE WITH: 0 *ProPoints* value green salad.

TIP: To transport this meal, place pasta mixture in an airtight container before adding the parmesan. Place parmesan in a snap-lock bag. Transport in a chiller bag and keep chilled until required. Reheat in microwave (if desired) and sprinkle with parmesan just before serving.

Chicken BLT

 ProPoints VALUES PER SERVE | SERVES: 2 | PREP: 15 MINS | COOKING TIME: 10 MINS

▲ **150g lean chicken breast, fat trimmed**
   2 slices (42g) Weight Watchers Bacon
   1 tbs Weight Watchers Mayonnaise
   2 tsp Dijon mustard
   4 x 35g slices wholegrain bread
▲ **2 iceberg lettuce leaves, chopped**
▲ **1 tomato, thinly sliced**

Filling & Healthy Foods are marked with a green triangle. These foods help fill you up and keep you healthy.

1 Lightly spray a medium non-stick frying pan with oil and heat over high heat. Cook chicken for 3–5 minutes each side or until cooked through. Transfer to a plate. Cover chicken with foil and set aside to rest for 5 minutes before slicing thinly.

2 Meanwhile, cook bacon in same pan for 1–2 minutes each side or until crisp.

3 Combine mayonnaise and mustard in a small bowl. Grill or toast the bread on both sides until lightly browned. Top 2 slices of toast with lettuce, tomato, bacon and chicken. Drizzle with mayonnaise mixture and sandwich with remaining toast. Cut in half to serve.

BY ADDING CHICKEN TO THIS EVER-POPULAR SANDWICH WE'VE MADE IT EVEN MORE FILLING. A DASH OF DIJON MUSTARD ALSO PROVIDES A SIMPLE YET DELICIOUS TWIST.

Polenta wedges with roast vegetable salad

 ProPoints VALUES PER SERVE | **SERVES: 6** | **PREP: 20 MINS** | **COOKING TIME: 40 MINS, PLUS 1 HOUR CHILLING**

2 cups (500ml) vegetable stock
▲ 1¼ cups (200g) yellow polenta
⅓ cup (25g) grated parmesan cheese
100g reduced-fat feta cheese, crumbled
▲ 400g Japanese pumpkin, unpeeled, cut into thin wedges
▲ 1 red capsicum, chopped
▲ 1 eggplant, cut into 3cm pieces
▲ 2 zucchini, thickly sliced
▲ 3 portobello mushrooms, thickly sliced (see note)
▲ 1 red onion, cut into thin wedges
1 tbs olive oil
2 tsp ground cumin
1 tsp ground coriander
1 tsp smoked paprika
¼ cup (75g) low-fat whole-egg mayonnaise
1 garlic clove, crushed
2 tsp lemon juice
▲ 5 cups (150g) baby spinach leaves

Filling & Healthy Foods are marked with a green triangle. These foods help fill you up and keep you healthy.

1 Line base and side of a 20cm round cake tin with foil. Bring stock and 2 cups (500ml) water to the boil in a large saucepan. Gradually stir in polenta. Cook, stirring, over low heat for 5–7 minutes or until very thick. Stir in parmesan and feta. Season with salt and freshly ground black pepper. Spoon into prepared tin and smooth the surface. Refrigerate for 1 hour or until firm.

2 Preheat oven to 200°C or 180°C fan-forced. Place pumpkin, capsicum, eggplant, zucchini, mushrooms and onion in 2 large baking dishes. Combine oil, cumin, coriander and paprika in a small jug. Drizzle oil mixture over vegies in both dishes and toss to coat. Bake for 25–30 minutes or until vegetables are golden and tender.

3 Meanwhile, lift polenta from pan and peel away foil. Cut polenta into 6 wedges. Line a large baking tray with baking paper. Place polenta on prepared tray and lightly spray with oil. Bake with vegetables for 10 minutes each side or until golden and crisp.

4 Combine mayonnaise, garlic, juice and 1 tablespoon hot water in a small bowl. Place roasted vegetables in a large bowl. Add spinach and toss gently to combine. Divide polenta wedges and salad among plates and serve drizzled with garlic mayonnaise.

NOTE: Portobello mushrooms are large, fully opened Swiss brown mushrooms and have a rich, earthy flavour. If unavailable you can use any large mushroom. The **ProPoints** values remain the same.

Grilled salmon salad

- ▲ ½ cup (100g) brown rice
  150g skinless boneless salmon fillets
- ▲ 75g sugar snap peas
- ▲ 100g cherry tomatoes, halved
- ▲ ½ Lebanese cucumber, thinly sliced
- ▲ ½ red capsicum, cut into thin strips
- ▲ 40g button mushrooms, thinly sliced
  1 tbs chopped fresh chives
  1 tbs lemon juice
  2 tsp balsamic vinegar
  2 tsp extra-virgin olive oil

Filling & Healthy Foods are marked with a green triangle.
These foods help fill you up and keep you healthy.

1 Cook rice in a large saucepan of boiling salted water, following packet instructions, or until just tender. Drain. Set aside to cool (see tip).

2 Meanwhile, preheat grill to high. Line grill tray with foil. Grill salmon for 3 minutes each side for medium or until cooked to your liking. Cool slightly. Use a fork to flake salmon into large chunks.

3 Place sugar snap peas in a medium heatproof bowl and cover with boiling water. Set aside for 2 minutes. Drain and refresh in a bowl of cold water. Drain.

4 Place rice, salmon, sugar snap peas, tomatoes, cucumber, capsicum, mushrooms and chives in a large bowl. Whisk juice, vinegar and oil in a small bowl. Add dressing to salad and toss gently to combine. Serve.

NOTE: You can cook the rice a day ahead. Store in an airtight container in the fridge until needed.

TIP: To take this to work, place salad, without dressing, in an airtight container. Pour dressing into a small snap-lock bag. Transport in a chiller bag and keep chilled until required. Drizzle with dressing just before serving.

Sweet potato patties with raita

ProPoints VALUES PER SERVE | SERVES: 4 | PREP: 15 MINS | COOKING TIME: 45 MINS, PLUS 10 MINS COOLING

- ▲ ½ cup (100g) red lentils
- ▲ 1 medium sweet potato (kumara), grated
  - 1 tsp ground coriander
  - 1½ tsp ground cumin
- ▲ ½ red onion, thinly sliced
  - ¼ cup fresh coriander leaves
- ▲ 1 egg, lightly beaten
  - 2 tbs plain flour
  - 1 tbs rice bran oil (see note)
- ▲ 2 Lebanese cucumbers, chopped
  - ¼ cup fresh mint leaves, chopped
- ▲ ½ cup (140g) low-fat natural yoghurt
  - 2 tbs lemon juice
- ▲ 2 cups (60g) mixed salad leaves
  - Lemon wedges, to serve

Filling & Healthy Foods are marked with a green triangle. These foods help fill you up and keep you healthy.

1 Place lentils in a medium saucepan. Cover with 1 cup (250ml) cold water and bring to the boil over high heat. Reduce heat to low and simmer for 20 minutes. Add sweet potato, ground coriander and half the cumin and cook for 2 minutes. Drain well and return to saucepan. Cool for 10 minutes. Add onion, fresh coriander, egg and flour and mix until well combined. Season with salt and freshly ground black pepper.

2 Heat oil in a medium non-stick frying pan over medium-low heat. Spoon ¼ cup (60ml) lentil mixture into pan and spread out with a spoon to 1cm thick. Cook for 2–3 minutes each side or until lightly browned and cooked through. Transfer to a plate. Cover to keep warm. Repeat with remaining lentil mixture to make 12 patties (you can cook 3–4 at once to save time).

3 Place cucumber, mint, yoghurt, juice and remaining cumin in a small bowl. Mix until raita is well combined. Serve patties with raita, salad leaves and lemon wedges.

NOTE: You can use sunflower or canola oil instead of rice bran oil. The *ProPoints* values remain the same.

Soba noodle & tuna salad

 ProPoints VALUES PER SERVE | SERVES: 2 | PREP: 10 MINS | COOKING TIME: 10 MINS

▲ **100g soba noodles**
▲ **2 x 150g tuna steaks**
1 tbs sesame seeds
▲ **1 cup (100g) snow peas, thinly sliced**
▲ **1 cup (55g) watercress sprigs**
▲ **1 cup (30g) baby spinach leaves**
▲ **2 green shallots, thinly sliced**
¼ cup fresh coriander leaves
2 tbs lemon juice
1 tbs soy sauce
1 tsp wasabi paste (see note)

Filling & Healthy Foods are marked with a green triangle.
These foods help fill you up and keep you healthy.

1 Cook noodles in a large saucepan of boiling water, following packet instructions, or until just tender. Refresh under cold water. Drain. Transfer to a large bowl.

2 Meanwhile, sprinkle 1 side of tuna steaks with sesame seeds. Lightly spray a medium non-stick frying pan with oil and heat over medium-high heat. Cook tuna for 2–3 minutes each side or until cooked to your liking. Slice thinly.

3 Add snow peas, watercress, spinach, shallots and coriander to noodles. Toss to combine. Whisk juice, soy sauce and wasabi in a small bowl until combined. Serve salad topped with tuna and drizzled with wasabi dressing.

NOTE: Wasabi is a hot, pungent condiment made from Japanese horseradish. It is sold in paste or powdered form in the Asian section of most supermarkets.

*TIP: You can use a 425g can of tuna in brine sprinkled with toasted sesame seeds instead of fresh tuna. The recipe will then have 11 **ProPoints** values per serve.*

Zucchini, corn & haloumi fritters

6 *ProPoints* VALUES PER SERVE | SERVES: 4 | PREP: 15 MINS | COOKING TIME: 15 MINS

▲ 1 small zucchini, grated
½ tsp salt
⅔ cup (100g) self-raising flour
1 tsp sumac (see note)
▲ ½ cup (125ml) skim milk
▲ 1 egg, separated
▲ ½ cup (90g) frozen corn kernels, thawed
100g reduced-fat haloumi cheese, grated
▲ 2 green shallots, thinly sliced, plus extra to garnish
▲ ⅓ cup (95g) low-fat Greek-style yoghurt
Lemon wedges, to serve

Filling & Healthy Foods are marked with a green triangle.
These foods help fill you up and keep you healthy.

1 Combine zucchini and salt in a colander set over a bowl. Set aside for 10 minutes to drain.

2 Meanwhile, sift flour and sumac into a medium bowl. Place milk and egg yolk in a small jug and mix until well combined. Make a well in the centre of flour mixture and pour in egg mixture. Whisk batter until smooth.

3 Using electric beaters, beat egg white in a clean, dry bowl until soft peaks form. Gently fold egg white into batter. Squeeze excess moisture from zucchini. Add to batter with corn, haloumi and sliced shallots and fold gently until combined.

4 Lightly spray a large non-stick frying pan with oil and heat over medium heat. Spoon heaped tablespoons of batter into pan and spread out with a spoon to 1cm thick. Cook for 2–3 minutes each side or until browned and cooked through. Transfer to a plate. Cover to keep warm. Repeat with remaining batter to make 12 fritters. Serve with yoghurt, extra shallots and lemon wedges.

NOTE: Sumac is a purple-red spice with a lemony flavour. It is available in the spice aisle of most supermarkets.

SERVE WITH: Salad made with 1 Lebanese cucumber (chopped), 2 tomatoes (chopped) and ½ thinly sliced red onion and 400g can of chickpeas (rinsed, drained). Add 2 *ProPoints* values per serve for chickpeas.

Chilli chicken wrap

ProPoints VALUES PER SERVE | SERVES: 1 | PREP: 10 MINS

▲ **60g cooked skinless lean chicken breast, shredded**
▲ **½ carrot, grated**
▲ **⅓ Lebanese cucumber, thinly sliced**
▲ **2 green shallots, thinly sliced**
  2 tsp sweet chilli sauce
  1 tsp flaxseed oil (see note)
  1 x 40g wholegrain wrap
▲ **½ cup (15g) rocket leaves**
  3 sprigs fresh coriander

Filling & Healthy Foods are marked with a green triangle. These foods help fill you up and keep you healthy.

1 Place chicken, carrot, cucumber and shallots in a medium bowl. Combine sweet chilli sauce and oil in a small bowl. Drizzle sauce mixture over chicken mixture and toss to combine.

2 Place wrap on a flat surface and top with rocket, chicken mixture and coriander. Roll to enclose filling. Serve.

NOTE: Flaxseed oil has a nutty flavour and is rich in essential fatty acids. It is sold in the health-food section of most supermarkets or health-food stores and should be stored in the fridge and not heated (it will damage the healthy fats). If unavailable you can use canola or sunflower oil. The ***ProPoints*** values remain the same.

TIP: To take this to work, place chicken mixture in an airtight container and sit the rocket and coriander on top. Place the wrap in a snap-lock bag or wrap in plastic wrap. Transport in a chiller bag and keep chilled until required. Assemble wrap at work.

Chicken, pumpkin & bean soup

 ProPoints VALUES PER SERVE | **SERVES: 8** | **PREP: 15 MINS** | **COOKING TIME: 30 MINS**

1 tbs olive oil
▲ 1 brown onion, finely chopped
2 garlic cloves, crushed
2 tbs tomato paste
1.5L (6 cups) chicken stock
▲ 1kg butternut pumpkin, cut into 2cm cubes
▲ 300g lean chicken breast fillet, fat trimmed,
thinly sliced
▲ 2 x 400g cans borlotti beans, rinsed, drained
▲ ½ bunch silverbeet

*Filling & Healthy Foods are marked with a green triangle.
These foods help fill you up and keep you healthy.*

1 Heat oil in a large saucepan over medium heat. Add onion and cook, stirring occasionally, for 5 minutes or until softened. Add garlic and cook, stirring, for 1 minute. Stir in tomato paste.

2 Add stock and pumpkin. Cover and bring to the boil. Reduce heat to low and simmer for 12–15 minutes or until the pumpkin is just tender.

3 Add chicken and cook for 5 minutes or until chicken is cooked through. Add beans and silverbeet and cook for 1 minute or until silverbeet is wilted. Ladle into bowls to serve.

SERVE WITH: Pesto toast. Grill or toast a 40g slice of sourdough bread until lightly browned. Spread with 1 teaspoon of basil pesto. Add 3 **ProPoints** values per serve per slice.

TIP: This soup is suitable to freeze. Ladle cooled soup into individual portion-sized airtight containers, leaving a 1–2cm gap at the top for expansion. Label, date and freeze for up to 2 months. Thaw in the fridge overnight before reheating in the microwave or a saucepan.

Quinoa, prosciutto & goat's cheese salad

ProPoints VALUES PER SERVE | SERVES: 4 | PREP: 20 MINS | COOKING TIME: 30 MINS

▲ **12 baby beetroot, peeled, halved**
   4 slices (60g) lean prosciutto, fat trimmed
▲ **1 cup (170g) white quinoa (see note)**
▲ **5 cups (150g) baby spinach leaves**
▲ **1 Lebanese cucumber, cut into 1cm pieces**
▲ **½ red onion, thinly sliced**
   100g goat's cheese, crumbled
   2 tbs red wine vinegar
   1 tbs extra-virgin olive oil
   1 tsp Dijon mustard
   4 x 25g slices ciabatta bread

Filling & Healthy Foods are marked with a green triangle.
These foods help fill you up and keep you healthy.

1 Preheat oven to 200°C or 180°C fan-forced. Lightly spray a baking tray with oil. Place beetroot on tray and lightly spray with oil. Bake for 20 minutes. Add prosciutto to tray. Bake for 10 minutes or until beetroot is tender and prosciutto is crisp. Coarsely chop prosciutto.
2 Meanwhile, place 2 cups (500ml) water in a medium saucepan over high heat and bring to the boil. Add quinoa. Reduce heat to low and simmer, covered, for 10–12 minutes or until water is absorbed. Drain.
3 Place spinach, cucumber, onion, cheese, beetroot, prosciutto and quinoa in a large bowl. Toss gently to combine. Whisk vinegar, oil and mustard in a small bowl until combined. Add dressing to salad and toss gently to combine. Grill or toast ciabatta on both sides until lightly browned. Serve with salad.
NOTE: Quinoa (say "keen-wah") is a tiny red or white seed and is a good substitute for rice. It is available in the health-food aisle of most supermarkets or from health-food stores.

THESE PITA POCKETS ARE FULL OF SURPRISES!
FROM SWEET CARROT AND SULTANAS TO
CUMIN-SPICED LAMB AND CORIANDER, THEY
TASTE AS GOOD AS THEY LOOK.

Lamb & hommus wholemeal pita

9 *ProPoints* VALUES PER SERVE | SERVES: 2 | PREP: 10 MINS | COOKING TIME: 10 MINS

 150g lean lamb backstrap (eye of loin), fat trimmed
1 tsp ground cumin
 2 carrots, grated
2 tbs sultanas
¼ cup fresh coriander leaves
1 x 60g wholemeal pita bread, halved
¼ cup (90g) reduced-fat hommus

Filling & Healthy Foods are marked with a green triangle. These foods help fill you up and keep you healthy.

1 Sprinkle lamb with cumin and season with salt and freshly ground black pepper.
2 Preheat a chargrill or barbecue over medium-high heat. Lightly spray lamb with oil and cook for 3–4 minutes each side for medium or until cooked to your liking. Transfer to a plate. Cover lamb with foil and set aside to rest for 5 minutes before slicing thinly.
3 Place carrot, sultanas and coriander in a medium bowl and toss to combine. Using your fingers, gently separate each pita half to form a pocket. Spread inside of each pita with hommus. Fill with carrot salad and sliced lamb. Serve.

TIP: You can use parsley or rocket leaves instead of coriander. The ProPoints values remain the same.

5 QUICK DINNER IDEAS

1 **Mustard lamb & vegies:** Chargrill 125g lamb fillet until seared. Toss fillet in 1 tsp each of Dijon mustard, balsamic vinegar and Worcestershire sauce. Bake 5–10 minutes to your liking. Serve with 3 roasted baby (chat) potatoes and 1 cup steamed vegies.

ProPoints VALUES PER SERVE | SERVES: 1 — 9

2 **Teriyaki pork:** Pan-fry 180g pork fillet (marinated in 1 tbs teriyaki sauce) to your liking. Serve with ½ cup cooked brown rice, mixed with pickled ginger (chopped) and fresh chives (sliced), plus 1 cup stir-fried mixed vegies (cook with spray oil and a little water).

ProPoints VALUES PER SERVE | SERVES: 1 — 8

3 **Salmon & salsa:** Grill 150g salmon fillet (skin-side down, without turning) to your liking. Serve with rocket leaves, ½–1 cup salsa (made with chopped tomatoes, capers, red onion, parsley, lemon juice and 1 tsp healthy oil) and ½ cup couscous.

ProPoints VALUES PER SERVE | SERVES: 1 — 11

4 **Steak & jacket potato:** Chargrill 130g beef fillet to your liking. Serve with 2 tsp Dijon mustard, 1 medium jacket potato topped with 1 tbs extra-light sour cream, plus 2 cups salad leaves, drizzled with 1 tsp each of olive oil and lemon juice.

ProPoints VALUES PER SERVE | SERVES: 1 — 8

5 **Dijon chicken:** Pan-fry 125g chicken breast until seared. Toss in 2 tsp Dijon mustard, 1 tbs lemon juice and 1 garlic clove (crushed). Bake 12 minutes or until cooked. Serve with ½ cup each of sweet potato mash, steamed carrots and wilted spinach.

ProPoints VALUES PER SERVE | SERVES: 1 — 8

Dinner

WHAT MAKES A GOOD DINNER?

At day's end it's great to sit down to a delicious meal. For a balanced dinner, try to include one serve of protein, one serve of starchy vegies or grain, three serves of cooked vegies, legumes or salad (or a combination of these), plus one teaspoon of healthy oil. Choose healthier cooking methods, such as poaching or grilling, and use herbs and spices to boost flavour.

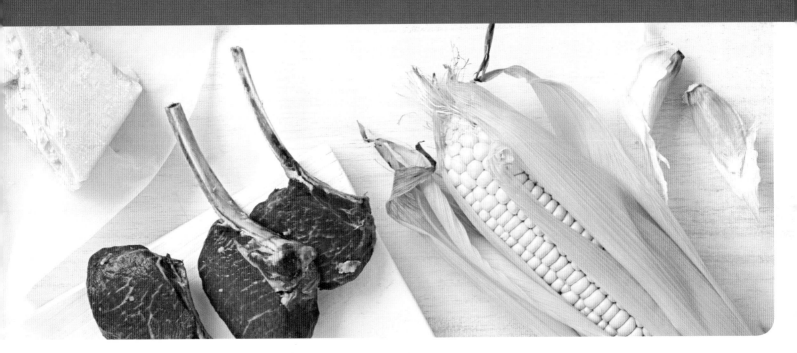

Barbecued sumac lamb with fattoush & baba ganoush

 ProPoints VALUES PER SERVE | SERVES: 6 | PREP: 25 MINS, PLUS 1 HOUR MARINATING
COOKING TIME: 45 MINS

2 tsp sumac
2 tsp finely grated lemon rind
½ cup (125ml) lemon juice
3 garlic cloves
1½ tbs olive oil
▲ 1kg butterflied leg of lamb, fat trimmed
(see note)
▲ 1 large eggplant
1 tbs tahini
1 x 68g wholemeal pita bread
▲ 2 Lebanese cucumbers, cut into 1cm pieces
▲ 3 tomatoes, cut into 1cm pieces
▲ 1 red onion, thinly sliced
1 cup fresh mint
¾ cup fresh coriander leaves
Lemon wedges, to serve

*Filling & Healthy Foods are marked with a green triangle.
These foods help fill you up and keep you healthy.*

1 Combine sumac, rind, 2 tablespoons juice, 1 garlic clove (crushed) and 2 teaspoons oil in a bowl. Place lamb in a large glass or ceramic dish and rub all over with sumac mixture. Season with salt and freshly ground black pepper. Cover and refrigerate for 1 hour.

2 Heat a covered barbecue to medium-high heat. Cook lamb for 5–7 minutes each side or until browned. Reduce heat to low. Cover and cook for 30–35 minutes or until cooked to your liking (see tip). Cover with foil and set aside to rest for 10 minutes before slicing thinly.

3 Meanwhile, pierce eggplant all over with a fork. Cook on barbecue grill plate, turning occasionally, for 15–20 minutes or until skin blackens and flesh is soft. Set aside for 10 minutes. Peel and discard skin. Place flesh in a colander to drain for 10 minutes. Place in a food processor or blender with 1 garlic clove (crushed), tahini, 2 tablespoons juice and 2 teaspoons oil. Process until smooth. Set baba ganoush aside.

4 Preheat grill on high. Grill pita for 1–2 minutes each side or until golden and crisp. Cool and break into 5cm pieces. Combine cucumber, tomatoes, onion, mint, coriander and remaining juice, garlic (crushed) and oil in a large bowl. Add pita crisps just before serving and gently toss fattoush to combine. Serve with lamb, baba ganoush and lemon wedges.

NOTE: You will need to buy a 1.4kg leg of lamb on the bone. Ask your butcher to butterfly it for you. Once the bone is removed you'll have 1kg butterflied leg of lamb. Trim as much fat as possible to give you a lean 800g piece of lamb.

TIP: You can cook the lamb in the oven instead of a covered barbecue. Preheat oven to 200°C or 180°C fan-forced. Place marinated lamb in a baking dish and bake for 20–30 minutes or until cooked to your liking.

Sweet potato, red onion & feta frittata

 ProPoints VALUES PER SERVE | SERVES: 6 | PREP: 15 MINS | HOUR 15 MINS

▲ **750g sweet potato (kumara), cut into 2cm pieces**
▲ **1 red onion, cut into thin wedges**
▲ **4 roma tomatoes, halved**
100g reduced-fat feta cheese, cut into 1cm pieces
1 tbs chopped fresh rosemary
▲ **6 eggs, lightly beaten**

Filling & Healthy Foods are marked with a green triangle. These foods help fill you up and keep you healthy.

1 Prehe... ...30°C fan-forced. Line 2 large baking trays wi... ...ge sweet potato on 1 prepared tray and ... ...th oil. Bake for 20 minutes. Add onion to tray. Bake for 20 minutes or until vegetables are tender and lightly browned. Cool for 5 minutes.

2 Place tomatoes on remaining prepared tray and lightly spray with oil. Bake for 30 minutes or until tender and lightly browned.

3 Meanwhile, place sweet potato mixture in a large bowl. Add feta and rosemary and season with freshly ground black pepper. Toss to combine. Lightly spray a 20cm (base measurement) round ovenproof baking dish with oil. Arrange sweet potato mixture over base of dish. Pour over egg, pressing vegetables down with a spatula to cover with egg. Bake in oven with tomatoes for 25–35 minutes or until golden and set.

4 Set frittata aside for 5 minutes. Cut into wedges and serve with roasted tomatoes.

SERVE WITH: 0 **ProPoints** value leafy green salad, sprinkled with basil leaves and drizzled with 1½ tablespoons extra-virgin olive oil and a little balsamic vinegar. Add 1 **ProPoints** value per serve for oil.

TIP: *Roasting the sweet potatoes and onion gives a rich caramelised flavour. If you're short on time you can steam or microwave the sweet potato until tender and cook the onion in a non-stick frying pan lightly sprayed with oil.*

Lamb shank broth with gremolata

 ProPoints VALUES PER SERVE | SERVES: 8 | PREP: 15 MINS | COOKING TIME: 2 HOURS 20 MINS

▲ 8 x 200g lean French-trimmed lamb shanks, fat trimmed

2 bay leaves

▲ ¾ cup (150g) brown rice

3 cups (750ml) beef stock

▲ 2 carrots, chopped

▲ 2 celery sticks, chopped

▲ 2 zucchini, chopped

▲ 2 tomatoes, chopped

▲ 1 cup (120g) frozen peas, thawed

1 cup fresh flat-leaf parsley leaves, coarsely chopped

1 garlic clove, crushed

1 tbs finely grated lemon rind

1 tbs olive oil

Filling & Healthy Foods are marked with a green triangle. These foods help fill you up and keep you healthy.

1 Place shanks and bay leaves in a large heavy-based saucepan over medium-high heat. Cover with water and bring to the boil. Reduce heat to low and simmer, covered, for 1½ hours or until meat is tender. Remove shanks from pan and set aside to cool slightly. Discard water. When cool enough to handle, remove meat from bones. Discard bones. Using 2 forks, roughly shred meat, discarding any fat.

2 Place rice, stock and 1L (4 cups) water in a large heavy-based saucepan over medium-high heat and bring to the boil. Reduce heat to low and simmer for 20 minutes.

3 Add carrot and celery and cook for 10 minutes. Return meat to broth with zucchini and tomatoes and cook for 6–8 minutes or until vegetables are tender. Add peas and cook for 2–3 minutes or until peas are tender.

4 Meanwhile, place parsley, garlic, rind and oil in a bowl. Mix gremolata until combined. Spoon broth into warmed serving bowls and serve sprinkled with gremolata.

TIP: This broth is suitable to freeze. Ladle cooled broth into individual portion-sized airtight containers, leaving a 1–2cm gap at the top for expansion. Label, date and freeze for up to 2 months. Thaw in the fridge overnight before reheating in the microwave or on the stovetop.

Baked mushroom & polenta chips

 11 *ProPoints* VALUES PER SERVE | SERVES: 4 | PREP: 20 MINS | COOKING TIME: 40 MINS, PLUS 1 HOUR REFRIGERATION

3 cups (750ml) vegetable stock
2 tsp fresh thyme leaves, plus extra sprigs to garnish
▲ 1 cup (170g) yellow polenta
▲ 4 large flat mushrooms
1 cup (70g) fresh breadcrumbs made from
    wholegrain bread
2 tbs finely chopped fresh flat-leaf parsley
2 garlic cloves, crushed
▲ 400g can cannellini beans, rinsed, drained
2 tbs pine nuts
⅓ cup (25g) finely grated parmesan cheese

Filling & Healthy Foods are marked with a green triangle.
These foods help fill you up and keep you healthy.

1 Preheat oven to 220°C or 200°C fan-forced. Line a baking tray with baking paper. Lightly spray a 20cm square cake tin with oil. Line base and sides with 1 sheet of baking paper, allowing it to hang over 2 sides.
2 Combine stock and thyme in a medium saucepan and bring to the boil. Gradually stir in polenta until smooth. Reduce heat to low and cook, stirring, for 3–4 minutes or until thick. Season with salt and freshly ground black pepper. Pour into prepared tin and smooth the surface. Refrigerate for 1 hour or until firm.
3 Lift polenta from tin and remove baking paper. Cut polenta lengthways into 8 even slices. Cut each slice in half crossways to make 16 fingers. Place on prepared tray and lightly spray with oil. Bake for 30 minutes or until golden and crisp.
4 Meanwhile, cut stalks from mushrooms and finely chop. Combine stalks, breadcrumbs, parsley, garlic, beans, pine nuts and parmesan in a bowl. Place mushrooms, top-side down, in a large baking dish. Spoon bean mixture onto mushrooms. Bake with polenta chips for 20 minutes or until mushrooms are golden and tender. Serve mushrooms with polenta chips and a sprig of thyme.
SERVE WITH: 0 *ProPoints* value garden salad.

Piri piri chicken with warm couscous salad

 ProPoints VALUES PER SERVE | **SERVES: 4** | **PREP: 25 MINS** | **COOKING TIME: 45 MINS**

- ▲ **1 carrot, cut into 2cm pieces**
- ▲ **500g butternut pumpkin, cut into 2cm pieces**
- ▲ **1 red capsicum, cut into 2cm pieces**
- ▲ **1 red onion, cut into 12 wedges**
- ▲ **2 zucchini, halved lengthways, cut into 2cm pieces**
- ▲ **2 x 300g lean chicken breast fillets, fat trimmed**
  2 tbs piri piri sauce
  ¾ cup (185ml) chicken stock
  ⅔ cup (125g) couscous
  1 tbs extra-virgin olive oil
  1 tbs lemon juice
- ▲ **400g can chickpeas, rinsed, drained**
  ⅓ cup fresh coriander leaves

Filling & Healthy Foods are marked with a green triangle.
These foods help fill you up and keep you healthy.

1 Preheat oven to 200°C or 180°C fan-forced. Line a large baking tray with baking paper. Spread carrot, pumpkin, capsicum, onion and zucchini on prepared tray and lightly spray with oil. Bake for 45 minutes or until tender and lightly browned. Cool to room temperature.

2 Meanwhile, cut chicken in half horizontally to make 4 flat pieces. Spread sauce over both sides of chicken and place on a plate. Cover loosely with plastic wrap and refrigerate until required.

3 Bring stock to the boil in a medium saucepan. Add couscous. Stir, cover and set aside for 5 minutes or until liquid has absorbed. Drizzle with oil and juice and scrape with a fork to separate grains. Transfer couscous mixture to a large bowl. Add chickpeas and roasted vegetables and toss gently to combine.

4 Preheat a chargrill or barbecue over medium-high heat. Cook chicken for 2–3 minutes each side or until cooked through. Cut each piece of chicken into 4 slices. Divide couscous salad among plates and top with chicken. Sprinkle with coriander to serve.

SERVE WITH: 0 **ProPoints** value baby rocket leaves, drizzled with 1 tablespoon each of extra-virgin olive oil and balsamic vinegar. Add 1 **ProPoints** value per serve for the oil.

Southern baked chicken with corn

 ProPoints VALUES PER SERVE | SERVES: 4 | PREP: 15 MINS | COOKING TIME: 15 MINS

3 tsp sweet paprika
½ tsp chilli powder
½ tsp dried sage
1 tsp caster sugar
▲ 600g lean chicken tenderloins, fat trimmed
▲ 1 egg, lightly beaten
2 garlic cloves, crushed
½ cup (50g) dried packaged breadcrumbs
▲ 2 corn cobs
2 limes, cut into wedges

Filling & Healthy Foods are marked with a green triangle.
These foods help fill you up and keep you healthy.

1 Preheat oven to 200°C or 180°C fan-forced. Line a large baking tray with baking paper. Combine paprika, chilli, sage and sugar in a bowl. Season with salt and freshly ground black pepper. Add chicken and toss to coat.
2 Whisk egg and garlic in a bowl until combined. Place breadcrumbs on a plate. Dip chicken in egg mixture, then toss in breadcrumbs to coat. Place chicken on prepared tray and lightly spray with oil. Bake for 15 minutes or until lightly browned and cooked through.
3 Meanwhile, boil, steam or microwave corn until tender. Cut corn into quarters and serve with chicken and lime wedges.
SERVE WITH: 0 *ProPoints* value steamed broccolini.

ONLY GOT HALF AN HOUR TO GET DINNER ON THE TABLE? THESE CRUNCHY CHICKEN TENDERS WITH A DASH OF SPICE CAN BE READY IN NO TIME.

Ginger poached tofu with udon noodles

 ProPoints VALUES PER SERVE | **SERVES: 4** | **PREP: 10 MINS** | **COOKING TIME: 20 MINS**

1.25L (5 cups) vegetable stock
5cm piece fresh ginger, thinly sliced
1 tbs soy sauce
▲ 1 bunch broccolini, cut into 5cm lengths
▲ 1 carrot, cut into ribbons (see tip)
▲ 1 bunch gai lan (Chinese broccoli), cut into
   5cm lengths
▲ 150g fresh shiitake mushrooms
200g pkt shelf-fresh udon noodles
▲ 350g firm tofu, cut into 2cm pieces
1 long fresh red chilli, thinly sliced
¼ cup fresh coriander leaves
1 tbs flaxseed oil (see note)

*Filling & Healthy Foods are marked with a green triangle.
These foods help fill you up and keep you healthy.*

1 Place stock, ginger, soy sauce and 2 cups (500ml) water in a large saucepan over high heat and bring to the boil. Reduce heat to low and simmer for 10 minutes.
2 Add broccolini, carrot, gai lan and mushrooms and cook for 2 minutes. Add noodles and tofu and cook for 2–3 minutes or until noodles are tender.
3 Ladle soup into warmed serving bowls. Top with chilli, and coriander. Drizzle with oil to serve.
NOTE: Flaxseed oil has a nutty flavour and is rich in essential fatty acids. It is sold in the health-food section of most supermarkets or health-food stores and should be stored in the fridge and not heated (it will damage the healthy fats). If unavailable you can use canola or sunflower oil. The **ProPoints** values remain the same.

TIP: *Use a vegetable peeler to cut carrot into thin ribbons.*

Mustard & brown sugar pork with coleslaw

 ProPoints VALUES PER SERVE | **SERVES: 4** | **PREP: 15 MINS, PLUS 3 HOURS MARINATING** | **COOKING TIME: 15 MINS**

2 tsp hot English mustard (see tip)
1 tbs brown sugar
1 tbs Worcestershire sauce
1 garlic clove, crushed
▲ 4 x 150g lean pork loin cutlets, fat trimmed
2 tbs Weight Watchers Mayonnaise
1 tbs lemon juice
1 tsp wholegrain mustard
▲ 3 cups (240g) shredded red cabbage
▲ 1 pink lady apple, unpeeled, thinly sliced
▲ 2 green shallots, thinly sliced
▲ 500g sweet potato (kumara), chopped
▲ 300g potatoes, chopped
½ cup (125ml) milk

*Filling & Healthy Foods are marked with a green triangle.
These foods help fill you up and keep you healthy.*

1 Combine English mustard, sugar, Worcestershire sauce and garlic in a shallow glass or ceramic bowl. Add pork and turn to coat. Cover and refrigerate for 3 hours.
2 Combine mayonnaise, juice and wholegrain mustard in a bowl. Place cabbage, apple and shallots in a large bowl. Add mayonnaise mixture and gently toss to combine. Set coleslaw aside.
3 Boil, steam or microwave sweet potato and potato until tender. Drain. Place in a large bowl with milk and mash until smooth. Season with salt and freshly ground black pepper.
4 Meanwhile, preheat a chargrill or barbecue over medium-high heat. Lightly spray pork with oil and cook for 3–5 minutes each side or until cooked to your liking. Cover with foil and set aside to rest for 5 minutes before serving.
5 Divide mash among plates and top with pork. Drizzle with resting juices and serve with coleslaw.

TIP: *You can use Dijon mustard instead of hot English mustard. The **ProPoints** values remain the same.*

Oven-steamed fish with Asian dressing

 ProPoints VALUES PER SERVE | SERVES: 4 | PREP: 10 MINS | COOKING TIME: 20 MINS

▲ **4 x 125g firm white fish fillets (see note)**
5cm piece fresh ginger, cut into thin matchsticks
2 long fresh red chillies, thinly sliced
▲ **5 green shallots, thinly sliced**
¼ cup (60ml) soy sauce
1 tbs sesame oil
▲ **1 bunch gai lan (Chinese broccoli), cut into**
10cm pieces
▲ **2 bunches broccolini, halved**
¼ cup fresh coriander leaves
2 cups (340g) steamed jasmine rice, to serve
Lime wedges, to serve

Filling & Healthy Foods are marked with a green triangle.
These foods help fill you up and keep you healthy.

1 Preheat oven to 180°C or 160°C fan-forced. Cut four 20cm-long pieces of baking paper. Place 1 fish fillet in the centre of each piece of paper. Top with ginger, chilli and shallots and drizzle with soy sauce. Fold paper to enclose filling and make a parcel. Tie with kitchen string and place on a baking tray. Bake for 20–25 minutes or until fish is cooked through.
2 Meanwhile, heat a wok over high heat. Add oil and heat for 5 seconds. Stir-fry gai lan and broccolini for 3–4 minutes or until tender.
3 Place fish parcels on plates. Carefully open paper and sprinkle fish with coriander. Serve with vegetables, rice and lime wedges.
NOTE: You can use any firm white fish fillets, such as snapper, blue-eye trevalla or ling.

Ricotta & lemon thyme-stuffed chicken

ProPoints 9 | *ProPoints* VALUES PER SERVE | SERVES: 4 | PREP: 15 MINS | COOKING TIME: 20 MINS

 500g potatoes, chopped
 1 cup (120g) frozen peas
100g reduced-fat fresh ricotta cheese
1 tsp finely grated lemon rind
1 tsp finely chopped fresh lemon thyme,
plus extra sprigs to garnish
1 garlic clove, crushed
 4 x 125g lean chicken breast fillets,
fat trimmed
 ⅓ cup (80ml) skim milk
1 tbs Weight Watchers Canola Spread
Lemon wedges, to serve

*Filling & Healthy Foods are marked with a green triangle.
These foods help fill you up and keep you healthy.*

1 Boil, steam or microwave potato and peas, separately, until tender.
2 Meanwhile, combine ricotta, rind, chopped thyme and garlic in a bowl. Cut a horizontal slit in the side of each chicken breast to form a pocket. Spoon ricotta mixture into pockets. Secure with wooden skewers or toothpicks.
3 Preheat a chargrill or barbecue over medium-high heat. Lightly spray chicken with oil. Cook for 5–6 minutes each side or until cooked through. Cover chicken with foil and set aside to rest for 5 minutes before slicing thickly.
4 Drain peas, reserving 1 tablespoon cooking liquid. Blend or process peas with reserved cooking liquid until almost smooth. Drain potato and place in a large bowl with milk and spread. Mash until smooth. Season with salt and freshly ground black pepper. Spoon pea mixture into mashed potato and use the end of a fork to gently swirl it through.
5 Divide mash among plates and top with chicken. Serve with thyme sprigs and lemon wedges.
SERVE WITH: 0 *ProPoints* value steamed vegetables, such as sugar snap peas, baby carrots, broccoli and yellow squash.

Tuscan pork fillet with cabbage salad

 ProPoints VALUES PER SERVE | SERVES: 4 | PREP: 15 MINS | COOKING TIME: 35 MINS

▲ **600g baby (chat) potatoes, halved**
2 tbs extra-virgin olive oil
2 tbs finely chopped fresh rosemary
1 tbs fennel seeds
1 tsp finely grated lemon rind
2 garlic cloves, crushed
Pinch chilli flakes
2 tsp honey
▲ **500g lean pork fillet, fat trimmed**
▲ **300g green cabbage, shredded**
▲ **2 carrots, shredded**
½ cup (40g) grated parmesan cheese
1 tbs balsamic glaze (see note)

Filling & Healthy Foods are marked with a green triangle.
These foods help fill you up and keep you healthy.

1 Preheat oven to 180°C or 160°C fan-forced. Place potato, half the oil and half the rosemary on a large baking tray and toss to combine. Roast for 35–40 minutes or until potato is golden and tender.

2 Meanwhile, using a mortar and pestle, crush fennel seeds, rind, garlic, chilli and remaining rosemary. Season with salt and freshly black pepper. Stir in honey. Rub mixture all over pork.

3 Lightly spray a medium non-stick frying pan with oil and heat over medium heat. Lightly spray pork with oil and cook, turning, for 4–5 minutes until browned. Transfer to a baking tray and bake with potatoes for 10–12 minutes or until cooked to your liking. Transfer to a plate. Cover pork with foil and set aside to rest for 5 minutes before slicing thickly.

4 Meanwhile, place cabbage, carrot, parmesan, remaining oil and balsamic glaze in a bowl. Stir to combine. Divide cabbage salad among plates and top with pork. Serve with roasted potatoes.

NOTE: Balsamic glaze is balsamic vinegar that has been sweetened with sugar and reduced until thick and syrupy. It is available in the gourmet aisle of some supermarkets or from specialty food stores.

Garlic lamb with honeyed vegetables

ProPoints VALUES PER SERVE | SERVES: 4 | PREP: 15 MINS | COOKING TIME: 30 MINS

- ▲ **500g parsnips, cut into thin wedges**
- ▲ **400g sweet potato (kumara), cut into thick batons**
- **1 tbs honey**
- **½ tsp ground cinnamon**
- **3 tsp olive oil**
- **1 garlic clove, crushed**
- ▲ **600g lean lamb backstrap (eye of loin), fat trimmed**
- ▲ **2 bunches English spinach, chopped**

*Filling & Healthy Foods are marked with a green triangle.
These foods help fill you up and keep you healthy.*

1 Preheat oven to 200°C or 180° fan-forced. Place parsnip, sweet potato, honey, cinnamon and half the oil in a bowl and toss to coat. Place mixture on a large baking tray and bake for 30–40 minutes or until tender and golden.

2 Meanwhile, combine remaining oil and garlic in a shallow glass or ceramic bowl. Add lamb and turn to coat. Lightly spray a large non-stick frying pan with oil and heat over medium-high heat. Cook lamb for 4–5 minutes each side for medium or until cooked to your liking. Transfer to a plate. Cover lamb with foil and set aside to rest for 5 minutes before slicing thickly.

3 Place spinach in a saucepan with ¼ cup (60ml) water and cook, covered, over high heat for 5 minutes or until wilted. Drain. Season with salt and freshly ground black pepper.

4 Serve lamb with spinach and honeyed vegetables.

Chicken goulash

ProPoints VALUES PER SERVE | SERVES: 4 | PREP: 20 MINS | COOKING TIME: 1 HOUR 5 MINS

¼ cup (35g) plain flour
 4 x 125g skinless chicken lovely legs, fat trimmed (see note)
▲ **4 x 125g skinless chicken thigh cutlets, fat trimmed**
1 tbs olive oil
▲ **1 brown onion, finely chopped**
2 garlic cloves, crushed
▲ **150g button mushrooms, quartered**
▲ **1 red capsicum, cut into 2cm pieces**
1½ tsp smoked paprika
1 tsp caraway seeds
1 tbs tomato paste
▲ **400g can diced tomatoes**
½ cup (125ml) chicken stock
250g large spiral pasta
2 tbs extra-light sour cream
1 tbs chopped fresh oregano

*Filling & Healthy Foods are marked with a green triangle.
These foods help fill you up and keep you healthy.*

1 Place flour in a plastic bag. Add chicken and toss to coat. Heat oil in a large saucepan over medium-high heat. Cook chicken, in batches, for 3–4 minutes or until browned. Remove from pan.
2 Lightly spray same pan with oil. Add onion and cook, stirring, for 3–5 minutes or until softened. Add garlic, mushrooms and capsicum and cook, stirring, for 2 minutes. Add paprika and caraway and cook for 1 minute.
3 Add tomato paste, tomatoes and stock and stir to combine. Return chicken to pan and bring to the boil. Reduce heat to low and simmer, covered, for 25 minutes. Uncover and simmer for 20 minutes or until chicken is cooked through.
4 Meanwhile, cook pasta in a large saucepan of boiling salted water, following packet instructions, or until just tender. Drain.
5 Divide goulash and pasta among plates. Top with sour cream and sprinkle with oregano to serve.
NOTE: Chicken lovely legs are drumsticks with the bones trimmed and skin removed. They are available from the meat section of most supermarkets or your local chicken shop.
SERVE WITH: 0 **ProPoints** value steamed spinach and/or green beans.

Chargrilled vegetables with ricotta & fennel salt

 ProPoints VALUES PER SERVE | SERVES: 4 | PREP: 15 MINS | COOKING TIME: 10 MINS

3 tsp fennel seeds
½ tsp sea salt flakes
½ tsp cracked black pepper
▲ 400g sweet potato (kumara), thinly sliced
▲ 1 red capsicum, cut into 4cm pieces
▲ 1 yellow capsicum, cut into 4cm pieces
▲ 2 zucchini, thinly sliced lengthways
▲ 2 roma tomatoes, halved
▲ 8 green shallots, halved
400g reduced-fat fresh ricotta cheese, crumbled
2 tbs flaxseed oil (see note)

Filling & Healthy Foods are marked with a green triangle. These foods help fill you up and keep you healthy.

1 Using a mortar and pestle, crush fennel seeds. Add sea salt and cracked black pepper and mix to combine.
2 Preheat a barbecue or chargrill over medium-high heat. Lightly spray sweet potato, capsicum, zucchini, tomatoes and shallots with oil and sprinkle with 2 teaspoons fennel salt. Cook, turning, for 8–10 minutes or until tender and lightly browned.
3 Place vegetables on a large serving platter and sprinkle with ricotta. Drizzle with flaxseed oil and sprinkle with remaining fennel salt. Serve.
NOTE: Flaxseed oil has a nutty flavour and is rich in essential fatty acids. It is sold in the health-food section of most supermarkets or health-food stores and should be stored in the fridge and not heated (it will damage the healthy fats).
If unavailable you can use canola or sunflower oil. The **ProPoints** values remain the same.
SERVE WITH: Steamed brown rice. Add 3 **ProPoints** values per serve for ½ cup (85g) cooked rice.

Spaghetti with fresh tomato sauce & bocconcini

 ProPoints VALUES PER SERVE | SERVES: 4 | PREP: 15 MINS | COOKING TIME: 15 MINS

275g spaghetti pasta
2 tsp olive oil
▲ **1 brown onion, thinly sliced**
2 garlic cloves, crushed
▲ **4 vine-ripened tomatoes, chopped**
8 (120g) baby bocconcini cheese, halved
⅓ cup fresh basil leaves

Filling & Healthy Foods are marked with a green triangle.
These foods help fill you up and keep you healthy.

1 Cook pasta in a large saucepan of boiling salted water, following packet instructions, or until just tender. Drain. Return pasta to pan.

2 Meanwhile, heat oil in a large non-stick frying pan over medium-high heat. Add onion and garlic and cook, stirring, for 5 minutes or until onion has softened. Add tomatoes and ½ cup (125ml) water and bring to the boil. Reduce heat and simmer, covered, for 15 minutes or until sauce has reduced slightly.

3 Add sauce and bocconcini to pasta and toss to combine. Serve sprinkled with basil and freshly ground black pepper.

SERVE WITH: 0 **ProPoints** value steamed green beans or asparagus, tossed in 1 teaspoon extra-virgin olive oil and sprinkled with 1 tablespoon shaved parmesan cheese. Add 1 **ProPoints** value per serve for oil and parmesan.

TIP: *Add bocconcini just before serving so it doesn't melt too much. You could use reduced-fat grated mozzarella cheese instead of bocconcini. The* **ProPoints** *values remain the same.*

Rosemary lamb cutlets with carrot rosti

 8 *ProPoints* VALUES PER SERVE | SERVES: 4 | PREP: 20 MINS | COOKING TIME: 45 MINS

- ▲ **2 potatoes**
- ▲ **2 carrots, halved**
- ▲ **1 egg, lightly beaten**
  1 tsp ground cumin
- ▲ **12 x 45g lean French-trimmed lamb cutlets, fat trimmed**
  2 tsp finely chopped fresh rosemary, plus extra sprigs to garnish

Filling & Healthy Foods are marked with a green triangle. These foods help fill you up and keep you healthy.

1 Preheat oven to 200°C or 180°C fan-forced. Line 2 large baking trays with baking paper.

2 Cook potatoes and carrot in a saucepan of boiling water for 5 minutes. Drain and cool slightly. Roughly grate potato and carrot into a large bowl. Add egg and cumin and stir until well combined. Shape ½ cup (125ml) mixture into a 9cm circle on 1 of the prepared trays. Repeat to make 8 rosti. Bake for 35–40 minutes or until rosti are golden and crisp.

3 Meanwhile, lightly spray lamb cutlets with oil and sprinkle with rosemary. Season with salt and freshly ground black pepper. Heat a chargrill or barbecue over medium-high heat. Cook cutlets for 2–3 minutes each side for medium or until cooked to your liking. Serve with carrot rosti and rosemary sprigs.

SERVE WITH: 0 *ProPoints* value steamed broccolini or sugar snap peas.

SUCCULENT STEAK AND ROAST POTATOES
ARE A WINNING COMBINATION. JUST ADD
AN INDIAN-STYLE RELISH AND YOU'VE
ENTERED THE 'WOW' ZONE.

Steak with eggplant relish & roast potatoes

7 *ProPoints* VALUES PER SERVE | SERVES: 4 | PREP: 15 MINS | COOKING TIME: 50 MINS

▲ **500g baby (chat) potatoes, halved**
1 tbs coarsely chopped fresh rosemary
½ tsp sea salt flakes
2 tsp olive oil
▲ **1 brown onion, finely chopped**
3 tsp tikka masala curry paste (see note)
▲ **1 eggplant, cut into 2cm pieces**
▲ **400g can crushed tomatoes**
2 tsp malt vinegar
2 tsp brown sugar
▲ **4 x 125g lean sirloin steaks, fat trimmed**

Filling & Healthy Foods are marked with a green triangle.
These foods help fill you up and keep you healthy.

1 Preheat oven to 200°C or 180°C fan-forced. Line a baking tray with baking paper.
2 Boil, steam or microwave potatoes until just tender. Drain. Place on prepared tray and lightly spray with oil. Sprinkle with rosemary and sea salt. Bake for 40 minutes or until crisp and golden.
3 Meanwhile, heat oil in a medium saucepan over medium heat. Add onion and cook, stirring, for 5 minutes or until softened. Add curry paste and cook for 1 minute. Add eggplant, tomatoes, vinegar and sugar. Bring to the boil. Reduce heat to low and simmer, covered, for 20 minutes or until eggplant is tender. Season relish with salt and freshly ground black pepper.
4 Preheat a barbecue or chargrill over medium-high heat. Lightly spray steaks with oil. Cook for 3–4 minutes each side for medium or until cooked to your liking. Transfer to a plate. Cover with foil and set aside to rest for 5 minutes before serving. Serve steaks with eggplant relish and roast potatoes.
NOTE: You can use korma, rogan josh or balti curry paste instead of tikka masala. The *ProPoints* values remain the same.
SERVE WITH: 0 *ProPoints* value steamed vegetables, such as asparagus, green beans, sugar snap peas and pumpkin.

Double-duty lasagne

 ProPoints VALUES PER SERVE | SERVES: 4 PER LASAGNE | PREP: 20 MINS | COOKING TIME: 1 HOUR 40 MINS

1 tbs olive oil

▲ 2 brown onions, finely chopped

4 garlic cloves, crushed

700g lean beef mince

▲ ½ cup (100g) red lentils, rinsed, drained

700g jar tomato passata sauce

1 cup (250ml) beef stock

3 tsp dried Italian herbs

3 tbs cornflour

▲ 3 cups (750ml) skim milk

¾ cup (90g) Bega So Extra Light 50% grated cheese

½ cup (50g) finely grated parmesan cheese

6 sheets (300g) fresh lasagne

Filling & Healthy Foods are marked with a green triangle. These foods help fill you up and keep you healthy.

1 Preheat oven to 180°C or 160°C fan-forced. Lightly spray two 20cm square (5cm-deep) ovenproof dishes with oil.

2 Heat oil in a large saucepan over medium heat. Add onion and cook, stirring, for 5 minutes or until softened. Add garlic and cook for 1 minute.

3 Lightly spray a large non-stick frying pan with oil and heat over high heat. Cook mince, in batches, stirring to break up lumps, for 3–5 minutes or until browned. Add to onion mixture with lentils, passata, stock and herbs. Bring to the boil. Reduce heat to low and simmer, covered, stirring occasionally, for 30 minutes or until lentils are soft.

4 Meanwhile, place cornflour in a bowl. Gradually stir in ¼ cup (60ml) milk until smooth. Place remaining milk in a saucepan and bring to the boil over medium heat. Gradually stir in cornflour mixture. Cook, stirring, until mixture boils and thickens. Combine both types of cheese in a bowl. Stir half the cheese mixture into the cornflour mixture.

5 Spread 1 cup (250ml) mince mixture over the base of each prepared dish. Top each with 1 lasagne sheet, trimming to fit. Spread each with ½ cup (125ml) cheese sauce. Continue layering with remaining mince mixture, lasagne sheets and cheese sauce, finishing with a layer of cheese sauce. Sprinkle both lasagnes with remaining cheese and bake for 50 minutes or until cooked through. Cool for 5 minutes. Serve.

SERVE WITH: 0 **ProPoints** value salad, made with baby English spinach, roasted pumpkin and thinly sliced red onion, drizzled with balsamic vinegar.

TIP: We have made 2 lasagnes so you can either serve 8 or freeze 1 for later. To freeze, allow cooked lasagne to cool and cover the surface with a piece of baking paper. Cover entire dish with 3 layers of plastic wrap and label, date and freeze for up to 3 months. Defrost in the fridge for 24 hours before reheating for 25–30 minutes in an oven preheated to 160°C or 140°C fan-forced.

Stir-fried scallops with Asian greens

 ProPoints VALUES PER SERVE | SERVES: 4 | PREP: 10 MINS | COOKING TIME: 10 MINS

1 tbs sesame oil
▲ 24 (312g) scallops, without roe
½ cup (125ml) hoisin sauce
2 tbs sweet chilli sauce
2 tbs light soy sauce
▲ 2 bunches gai lan (Chinese broccoli),
   cut into 5cm lengths
▲ 200g snow peas
▲ ¼ cup (50g) canned sliced bamboo shoots
▲ 2 green shallots, cut into 5cm lengths
2 cups (340g) steamed jasmine rice, to serve
2 tbs fried shallots (see note)

Filling & Healthy Foods are marked with a green triangle. These foods help fill you up and keep you healthy.

1 Heat a wok over medium-high heat. Add oil and heat for 5 seconds. Stir-fry scallops, in batches, for 2–3 minutes or until lightly browned. Transfer to a plate.
2 Add hoisin, sweet chilli and soy sauces and gai lan to wok and stir-fry for 2 minutes. Add snow peas, bamboo shoots and shallots and stir-fry for 2 minutes or until vegetables are tender. Return scallops to wok and stir-fry for 1 minute or until heated through.
3 Divide rice among plates and top with stir-fry. Serve sprinkled with fried shallots.
NOTE: Fried shallots are available in the Asian section of most supermarkets or from Asian grocery stores.

Lemon squid with Mediterranean salad

 ProPoints VALUES PER SERVE | SERVES: 4 | PREP: 10 MINS | COOKING TIME: 10 MINS

- ▲ 1 eggplant, thinly sliced
- ▲ 1 red capsicum, cut into 8 pieces
- 1 tbs rice bran oil (see note)
- 1 garlic clove, crushed
- 1 long fresh red chilli, thinly sliced
- ▲ 600g cleaned squid hoods (calamari), cut into triangles
- 2 tbs lemon juice
- ▲ 2 zucchini, cut into ribbons
- ▲ 100g snow peas, thinly sliced
- ▲ 4 cups (120g) mixed salad leaves
- ¼ cup fresh coriander leaves
- ¼ cup fresh mint
- 2 cups (340g) steamed brown rice, to serve

Filling & Healthy Foods are marked with a green triangle. These foods help fill you up and keep you healthy.

1 Lightly spray both sides of eggplant and capsicum with oil. Heat a large non-stick frying pan over medium heat. Cook eggplant, in batches, for 3–4 minutes each side or until lightly browned. Transfer to a plate. Add capsicum to pan and cook, turning, for 3–4 minutes or until lightly browned. Add to eggplant.

2 Heat oil in same cleaned pan over high heat. Add garlic, chilli and squid and cook, tossing, for 1–2 minutes or until squid is just cooked through. Add lemon juice and toss to coat. Set pan aside and cover to keep warm.

3 Place eggplant, capsicum, zucchini, snow peas, salad leaves, coriander and mint in a large bowl and toss to combine. Divide salad and rice among serving plates. Top with squid mixture. Drizzle with pan juices. Serve.

NOTE: Rice bran oil has a high smoke point, so it won't burn at high heat. It has a subtle, nutty taste that complements the delicate flavours of the squid.
If unavailable you can use canola or sunflower oil.
The **ProPoints** values remain the same.

Seafood hot-pot

ProPoints VALUES PER SERVE | **SERVES: 4** | **PREP: 10 MINS** | **COOKING TIME: 25 MINS**

1.5L (6 cups) fish stock
2 kaffir lime leaves, torn
1 tbs fish sauce
▲ 250g skinless snapper fillets, cut into
   5cm pieces
▲ 2 bunches broccolini, cut into 5cm lengths
▲ 100g snow peas
▲ 100g sugar snap peas
▲ 1 red capsicum, thinly sliced
▲ 300g large peeled green prawns,
   deveined, tails intact (see note)
▲ 150g scallops, without roe
½ cup (125ml) light coconut milk
150g rice vermicelli noodles
¼ cup fresh coriander leaves
Lime wedges, to serve

Filling & Healthy Foods are marked with a green triangle.
These foods help fill you up and keep you healthy.

1 Place stock, lime leaves and fish sauce in a large saucepan and bring to the boil over high heat. Reduce heat to low and simmer for 10 minutes. Add fish and cook for 5 minutes.
2 Add broccolini, snow peas, sugar snap peas and capsicum and cook for 2–3 minutes or until just tender. Add prawns, scallops and coconut milk and cook for 3–4 minutes or until seafood is just cooked through.
3 Meanwhile, place noodles in a heatproof bowl and cover with boiling water. Set aside for 3–5 minutes or until softened. Drain.
4 Divide noodles among serving bowls. Top with seafood and vegetables and ladle over broth. Sprinkle with coriander. Serve with lime wedges.
NOTE: You can find frozen peeled green (raw) prawns with tails intact (also known as prawn cutlets) in the freezer section of most supermarkets.

GO DIVING FOR FISH, PRAWNS AND
SCALLOPS AMONG THE VEGIES AND
NOODLES IN THIS DELICATE COCONUT
BROTH INFUSED WITH A HINT OF LIME.

THE ULTIMATE COMFORT FOOD. THIS
AUTHENTIC ITALIAN SAUCE IS SLOW-COOKED
UNTIL THE MEAT IS SO TENDER
IT ALMOST MELTS IN YOUR MOUTH.

Pasta with beef ragu

 ProPoints VALUES PER SERVE | SERVES: 4 | PREP: 15 MINS | COOKING TIME: 2 HOURS 20 MINS

1 tbs olive oil
▲ 400g lean beef chuck steak, fat trimmed, cut into 3cm pieces
▲ 1 brown onion, finely chopped
▲ 1 carrot, finely chopped
▲ 1 celery stick, finely chopped
1 garlic clove, thinly sliced
2 anchovy fillets, drained, chopped
1 tbs baby capers in brine, drained, chopped
1 cup (250ml) beef stock
▲ 400g can diced tomatoes
250g rigatoni pasta

*Filling & Healthy Foods are marked with a green triangle.
These foods help fill you up and keep you healthy.*

1 Heat oil in a large saucepan over medium-high heat. Cook steak, in batches, for 5 minutes or until browned. Transfer to a plate. Add onion, carrot and celery and cook, stirring, for 5 minutes or until softened. Add garlic, anchovies and capers and cook, stirring, for 1 minute.
2 Return beef to pan with stock and tomatoes and bring to the boil. Reduce heat to low and simmer, covered, for 1½ hours. Uncover and simmer for 30 minutes or until beef is tender and sauce slightly thickened. Using 2 forks, coarsely shred beef.
3 Meanwhile, cook pasta in a large saucepan of boiling salted water, following packet instructions, or until just tender. Drain. Return pasta to pan.
4 Add ragu to pasta and toss gently to combine. Serve.
SERVE WITH: 0 **ProPoints** value steamed green beans.
You can also serve the ragu on toast instead of pasta. The recipe will then be 7 **ProPoints** values per serve with a 35g slice of wholegrain toast.

TIP: You could make double the ragu and freeze half for later. Cool ragu and place in an airtight container, allowing 1–2cm at the top for expansion. Label, date and freeze for up to 3 months. Defrost overnight in the fridge and reheat in the microwave or on the stovetop.

Salmon & sweet potato patties

 ProPoints VALUES PER SERVE | SERVES: 4 | PREP: 20 MINS | COOKING TIME: 25 MINS, PLUS 10 MINS COOLING

- ▲ 500g sweet potato (kumara), chopped
- ▲ ⅔ cup (80g) frozen peas
- 2 x 150g skinless salmon fillets
- 5cm strip lemon rind
- 1⅓ cups (95g) fresh breadcrumbs made from white bread
- ▲ 1 egg, lightly beaten
- ▲ 2 green shallots, thinly sliced
- Lemon wedges, to serve

Filling & Healthy Foods are marked with a green triangle. These foods help fill you up and keep you healthy.

1 Boil, steam or microwave potato and peas, separately, until just tender. Drain. Place potato in a large bowl and mash until smooth. Stir in peas and set aside to cool.

2 Meanwhile, place salmon and lemon rind in a medium saucepan. Cover with water. Bring to the boil over medium heat. Reduce heat to low and simmer, covered, for 8–10 minutes or until salmon is just cooked through. Drain. Discard lemon rind. Cool salmon for 10 minutes. Using a fork, flake salmon into small pieces.

3 Add salmon, ⅓ cup breadcrumbs, egg and shallots to potato mixture and mix to combine. Place remaining breadcrumbs on a plate. Shape ⅓ cup (80ml) mixture into a 2cm-thick patty. Roll in breadcrumbs to coat. Repeat to make 8 patties. Lightly spray with oil.

4 Lightly spray a large non-stick frying pan with oil and heat over medium heat. Cook patties, in batches, for 2–3 minutes each side or until golden. Serve with lemon wedges

SERVE WITH: 0 **ProPoints** value baby rocket leaves with capsicum and walnut salsa. For salsa, combine 1 red capsicum (finely chopped), 1 yellow capsicum (finely chopped), 2 tomatoes (finely chopped), ½ small red onion (finely chopped), ¼ cup finely chopped basil, 2 tbs finely chopped walnuts, 1 tablespoon olive oil and 1 tablespoon white balsamic vinegar in a bowl and toss to combine. Add 2 **ProPoints** values per serve for the salsa.

Middle Eastern beef meatballs

 ProPoints VALUES PER SERVE | SERVES: 4 | PREP: 15 MINS | COOKING TIME: 30 MINS, PLUS 5 MINS COOLING

▲ **2 brown onions, finely chopped**
2 garlic cloves, crushed
450g lean beef mince
1 tsp ground cumin
½ tsp ground cinnamon
½ tsp allspice
2 tbs chopped fresh flat-leaf parsley
1 tbs olive oil
1½ tbs harissa paste
▲ **400g can chopped tomatoes**
1 cup (250ml) beef stock
▲ **2 carrots, grated**
▲ **2 zucchini, grated**
½ cup tabouli
▲ **2 cups (60g) baby rocket leaves**
1 tbs pine nuts, toasted
▲ **¼ cup (40g) low-fat Greek-style yoghurt**
2 x 80g rounds wholemeal Lebanese bread, torn

Filling & Healthy Foods are marked with a green triangle. These foods help fill you up and keep you healthy.

1 Lightly spray a medium non-stick frying pan with oil and heat over medium-high heat. Add half the onion and garlic and cook, stirring, for 3–4 minutes or until onion has softened. Cool for 5 minutes.
2 Place mince, onion mixture, cumin, cinnamon, allspice and parsley in a bowl. Mix to combine. Roll tablespoons of mixture into meatballs. Refrigerate for 10 minutes.
3 Meanwhile, heat oil in a saucepan over medium heat. Add remaining onion and garlic and cook, stirring, for 5 minutes or until onion has softened. Stir in harissa, tomatoes and stock and bring to the boil. Boil for 2 minutes.
4 Add carrot, zucchini and meatballs. Reduce heat to low and simmer, covered, for 15–20 minutes or until meatballs are cooked through and sauce has thickened.
5 Combine tabouli and rocket in a large bowl and toss to combine. Divide meatball mixture among plates and top with pine nuts and yoghurt. Serve with tabouli salad and bread.

FOR PURE DINNER DELIGHT WE'VE
TEAMED A TENDER BEEF FILLET WITH
A TASTY POTATO BAKE FLAVOURED
WITH FRESH THYME.

Roast beef with potato bake

 11 *ProPoints* VALUES PER SERVE | SERVES: 4 | PREP: 20 MINS | COOKING TIME: 1 HOUR

▲ **600g potatoes, thinly sliced**
▲ **1 brown onion, thinly sliced**
 ½ cup (125ml) chicken stock
 1 tsp fresh thyme leaves
▲ **600g lean beef fillet, fat trimmed**
 2 tsp olive oil
▲ **100g eschalots, thinly sliced**
 1 garlic clove, crushed
 ⅓ cup (80ml) red wine
 1 cup (250ml) beef stock
 2 tsp red wine vinegar
 10g butter
 Pinch brown sugar

Filling & Healthy Foods are marked with a green triangle.
These foods help fill you up and keep you healthy.

1 Preheat oven to 200°C or 180°C fan-forced. Lightly spray a 20cm square ovenproof dish with oil. Arrange one-third of the potato over base of dish, overlapping slices slightly. Spread half the onion over the potato. Repeat layering with remaining potato and onion, finishing with a layer of potato.
2 Pour stock into dish and sprinkle with thyme. Season with salt and freshly ground black pepper. Cover with foil and bake for 20 minutes. Uncover, lightly spray top with oil and bake for 40 minutes or until potato is crisp and golden.
3 Meanwhile, lightly spray a flameproof baking dish with oil and heat over medium-high heat. Cook beef, turning, for 3–5 minutes or until browned. Season with salt and freshly ground black pepper. Bake for 20 minutes for medium-rare or until cooked to your liking. Transfer to a plate. Cover with foil and set aside to rest for 5 minutes before slicing thickly.
4 Place baking dish (with remaining juices) and oil over medium heat. Add eschalots and cook, stirring, for 5 minutes or until softened. Add garlic and cook for 1 minute. Add wine and cook for 2 minutes or until reduced slightly. Stir in stock and bring to the boil. Reduce heat and simmer for 5 minutes or until thickened. Stir in vinegar, butter and sugar. Season with salt and freshly ground black pepper.
5 Divide potato bake and beef among plates and serve drizzled with sauce.
SERVE WITH: 0 *ProPoints* value steamed vegetables, such as baby carrots, zucchini and peas. Add 1 *ProPoints* value per serve for ½ cup (60g) peas.

5 QUICK DESSERT IDEAS

1 *Orange with almond yoghurt:* Cut 1 orange (peeled) into 1cm-thick slices. Serve with 50g 97% fat-free honey yoghurt or 150g diet yoghurt and 1 tbs toasted flaked almonds.

2 *Ricotta-stuffed dates:* Cut a slit in 2 fresh dates (pitted) and fill with 40g reduced-fat fresh ricotta cheese.

3 *Caramelised fruit:* Sprinkle 1 fresh nectarine, peach, apricot, fig or plum (halved) with 2 tsp sugar. Grill until top starts to caramelise slightly. Serve with 1 tsp chopped walnuts and 50g 97% fat-free honey yoghurt.

4 *Saucy poached pears:* Poach 1 pear (unpeeled) in a saucepan of simmering water with 1 cinnamon stick and 1 vanilla pod for 10 minutes or until tender. Serve with 1 tbs diet chocolate or caramel ice-cream topping and 1 tbs reduced-fat cream.

5 *Banana split:* Top 1 banana (split lengthways) with 12 (12g) toffee-coated or plain unsalted peanuts (chopped), 1 tbs sugar-free maple-flavoured syrup and ¼ cup (60g) diet vanilla yoghurt.

ProPoints 3 *ProPoints* VALUES PER SERVE | SERVES: 1

ProPoints 2 *ProPoints* VALUES PER SERVE | SERVES: 1

ProPoints 3 *ProPoints* VALUES PER SERVE | SERVES: 1

ProPoints 1 *ProPoints* VALUE PER SERVE | SERVES: 1

ProPoints 3 *ProPoints* VALUES PER SERVE | SERVES: 1

Dessert

CAN I STILL ENJOY DESSERT?

Yes. Dessert is a great way to include fruit and dairy serves from the Good Health Guidelines into your meals, and to enjoy a few healthy nuts. Allowing for treats is also a great way to motivate us to continue losing or maintaining weight. Fruit-based desserts are the best everyday choices, while more decadent sweets can be savoured for special occasions.

Chocolate cherry dessert cup

 ProPoints VALUES PER SERVE | **SERVES: 4** | **PREP: 10 MINS** | **COOKING TIME: 10 MINS**

▲ **300g frozen cherries, slightly thawed**
  1 tbs caster sugar
  4 x 50g scoops low-fat vanilla ice-cream
  2 tbs shredded coconut, toasted (see note)
  20g dark chocolate, shaved

*Filling & Healthy Foods are marked with a green triangle.
These foods help fill you up and keep you healthy.*

1 Combine cherries, sugar and 2 tablespoons water in a small saucepan over medium heat. Cook, covered, stirring occasionally, for 8–10 minutes or until cherries have softened. **2** Divide cherry mixture among serving glasses. Top with ice-cream. Serve sprinkled with coconut and chocolate. **NOTE:** To toast coconut, preheat oven to 200°C or 180°C fan-forced. Spread coconut on a baking tray and bake for 3 minutes or until toasted.

*TIP: You can use frozen or fresh raspberries, strawberries or blackberries instead of cherries. The **ProPoints** values remain the same.*

GENTLY POACHED CHERRIES ARE TOPPED
WITH ICE-CREAM AND A SPRINKLING OF
COCONUT AND CHOCOLATE IN THIS
ELEGANT YET EFFORTLESS DESSERT.

Banana & passionfruit ice-cream

 ProPoints VALUES PER SERVE | **SERVES: 6** | **PREP: 20 MINS, PLUS 3 HOURS FREEZING**

▲ **4 ripe frozen bananas (see tip)**
   2 tsp lemon juice
   500ml low-fat vanilla ice-cream
▲ **¼ cup (60ml) passionfruit pulp (see note)**
▲ **100g strawberries, halved**

Filling & Healthy Foods are marked with a green triangle.
These foods help fill you up and keep you healthy.

1 Place bananas and juice in a food processor and process until smooth. Add ice-cream and process until combined. Transfer to a large bowl. Stir in passionfruit pulp.
2 Pour banana mixture into a 1.5-litre capacity freezerproof dish. Cover with foil and freeze for 3 hours or until firm. Serve ice-cream in scoops topped with strawberries.
NOTE: You will need 1–2 fresh passionfruit for this recipe. If unavailable you can used tinned passionfruit. The **ProPoints** values remain the same.

TIP: You can freeze ripe bananas in snap-lock bags or an airtight container for up to 3 months. They are also handy for making cakes and muffins.

BY ADDING YOUR OWN DELICIOUS FRUIT YOU CAN EASILY TRANSFORM SIMPLE STORE-BOUGHT ICE-CREAM INTO A LIGHT AND DREAMY GOURMET TREAT.

Orange blossom panna cotta with rhubarb

ProPoints VALUES PER SERVE | SERVES: 4 | PREP: 25 MINS | COOKING TIME: 15 MINS, PLUS COOLING & 4 HOURS SETTING

▲ **½ cup (125ml) skim milk**
¼ cup (55g) caster sugar
2 tsp gelatine powder
500g tub low-fat Greek-style yoghurt
2 tsp orange blossom water (see tip)
▲ **4 rhubarb stalks, cut into 5cm lengths**
1 tsp finely grated orange rind
2 tbs orange juice

*Filling & Healthy Foods are marked with a green triangle.
These foods help fill you up and keep you healthy.*

1 Lightly spray four ¾-cup (185ml) capacity cups or metal moulds with oil. Place milk and sugar (reserve 1 tablespoon for later) in a small saucepan over medium heat. Stir until sugar has dissolved. Bring to the boil and remove from heat. Sprinkle gelatine over milk mixture and whisk until gelatine has dissolved. Transfer to a medium heatproof jug. Cool to room temperature.
2 Add yoghurt and orange blossom water to milk mixture and whisk until smooth. Pour mixture into prepared cups or moulds and cover with plastic wrap. Refrigerate for 4 hours or until set.
3 Meanwhile, place rhubarb, reserved sugar, rind and juice in a medium saucepan over medium heat. Cover and bring to the boil. Reduce heat to low and simmer for 4–5 minutes or until rhubarb is tender. Transfer to a bowl. Cool.
4 Dip each cup or mould briefly in hot water and turn panna cottas onto serving plates. Serve topped with rhubarb mixture.

TIP: *Popular in Middle Eastern sweets and desserts, orange blossom water (also known as orange flower water) is a concentrated citrus flavouring made from orange blossoms. It is available from gourmet food stores, delicatessens and Middle Eastern grocery outlets.*

Chocolate & pear tart

3 *ProPoints* VALUES PER SERVE | SERVES: 4 | PREP: 15 MINS | COOKING TIME: 25 MINS

▲ **1 large pear, peeled**
1 sheet reduced-fat puff pastry, just thawed
25g dark chocolate, chopped
2 tsp Weight Watchers Canola Spread, melted
1 tsp demerara sugar (see note)

Filling & Healthy Foods are marked with a green triangle.
These foods help fill you up and keep you healthy.

1 Preheat oven to 200°C or 180°C fan-forced. Line a tray with baking paper.
2 Cut pear into quarters and remove the core. Cut each quarter into 4 slices. Using a 9cm round pastry cutter, cut 4 rounds from pastry sheet. Place on prepared tray. Sprinkle chocolate onto the centre of each pastry round. Top each with 4 slices of pear.
3 Brush pears with melted spread and sprinkle with sugar. Bake for 25–30 minutes or until pastry is puffed and golden. Serve.
NOTE: Demerara is a coarse, golden sugar that creates a toffee-like crust when baked. It is available in the baking aisle of most supermarkets.

TIP: You can use sliced banana instead of pear.
*The **ProPoints** values remain the same.*

Spiced rice pudding with poached pear

 ProPoints VALUES PER SERVE | SERVES: 4 | PREP: 15 MINS | COOKING TIME: 30 MINS

½ cup (100g) arborio rice
▲ 2 cups (500ml) skim milk
2 tbs caster sugar
1 tsp ground cinnamon
2 vanilla pods, split, seeds scraped (see tip)
▲ 4 pears, peeled
2 tbs honey

*Filling & Healthy Foods are marked with a green triangle.
These foods help fill you up and keep you healthy.*

1 Place rice, milk, sugar, cinnamon, half the vanilla seeds and 1 split pod in a medium saucepan over medium-high heat. Bring to the boil. Reduce heat to low and cook, covered, stirring occasionally, for 25–30 minutes or until rice is tender. Remove vanilla pod.

2 Meanwhile place pears, honey, remaining vanilla seeds and pod in a medium saucepan. Add enough water to cover pears and place over medium-high heat. Bring to the boil. Reduce heat to low and cover surface with a round of baking paper (see note). Simmer for 20–25 minutes or until pears are tender. Drain pears and discard pod.

3 Divide spiced rice pudding among bowls and serve with poached pear.

NOTE: The baking paper is called a cartouche and it stops the pears from turning brown during cooking by helping them stay submerged in the poaching liquid.

TIP: Use a sharp knife to cut vanilla pods in half, then use the tip of the knife to scrape out the tiny seeds. Used vanilla pods can be rinsed, allowed to dry and then added to a jar of caster sugar to add extra flavour to cakes and muffins.

DISCOVER HOW EASY IT IS TO POACH FRESH FRUIT WITH THIS EASY RECIPE. IT'S GREAT ON ITS OWN AND EVEN BETTER WHEN TEAMED WITH CREAMY RICE PUDDING.

Apricot bread & butter custard

 ProPoints VALUES PER SERVE | **SERVES: 4** | **PREP: 15 MINS** | **COOKING TIME: 20 MINS**

6 x 40g slices day-old white bread,
   crusts removed
2 tbs apricot jam
¼ cup (45g) diced dried apricots
▲ 1 cup (250ml) skim milk
▲ 2 eggs
1 tbs caster sugar
1 tsp vanilla essence
1 tbs flaked almonds
1 tsp icing sugar, to dust

*Filling & Healthy Foods are marked with a green triangle.
These foods help fill you up and keep you healthy.*

1 Preheat oven to 180°C or 160°C fan-forced. Spread each slice of bread with jam and cut into 4 triangles. Press half the bread into four ½-cup (125ml) capacity ovenproof dishes and place on a baking tray. Sprinkle dried apricots over bread in dishes.

2 Whisk milk, eggs, caster sugar and essence in a jug until combined. Pour half the egg mixture over bread and apricots. Top with remaining bread and gradually pour over remaining egg mixture, allowing it to soak into the bread.

3 Sprinkle with almonds and bake for 20–25 minutes or until custard is set and golden. Serve dusted with icing sugar.

Apple strudel

3 *ProPoints* VALUES PER SERVE | SERVES: 6 | PREP: 20 MINS | COOKING TIME: 35 MINS

¾ tsp ground cinnamon
½ tsp ground ginger
1½ tbs caster sugar
▲ 2 granny smith apples, peeled, thinly sliced
1 tsp lemon juice
1 cup (70g) breadcrumbs made from fresh
   white bread
4 sheets filo pastry (see note)
2 tbs Weight Watchers Canola Spread, melted

Filling & Healthy Foods are marked with a green triangle.
These foods help fill you up and keep you healthy.

1 Preheat oven to 200°C or 180°C fan-forced. Line a baking tray with baking paper. Combine cinnamon, ginger and sugar in a small bowl.
2 Place apples in a medium bowl. Add juice and toss to coat. Drain apple mixture and discard juice. Reserve ½ tsp spice mix. Add remaining spice mixture and breadcrumbs to apples and toss to coat.
3 Place 1 sheet of filo on a flat surface and lightly brush with spread. Top with another sheet of filo and lightly brush with spread. Repeat with remaining filo to make a rectangular stack (leave some spread for Step 4). Arrange apple mixture along 1 short side of filo (see tip), leaving a 4cm border at each end. Roll filo to enclose filling.
4 Place strudel, seam-side down, on prepared tray and brush with remaining spread. Sprinkle with reserved spice mixture. Bake for 35–40 minutes or until golden. Cut into thick slices to serve.
NOTE: Fresh filo pastry sold in the chiller cabinets of most supermarkets is easier to work with and less likely to break than the frozen filo sold in the freezer cabinets.

TIP: Arrange apple mixture in an even mound when placing on pastry. This will help the strudel keep an even shape when cooked.

Fresh date & banana pudding

5 *ProPoints* VALUES PER SERVE | SERVES: 4 | PREP: 15 MINS | COOKING TIME: 20 MINS

8 fresh dates, pitted, chopped
 1 ripe banana, mashed
2 x 62g tubs NESTLÉ SOLEIL DIET Chocolate
  Mousse
▲ 2 eggs
¾ cup (105g) self-raising flour
⅓ cup (80ml) diet chocolate ice-cream
  topping

Filling & Healthy Foods are marked with a green triangle.
These foods help fill you up and keep you healthy.

1 Preheat oven to 200°C or 180°C fan-forced. Lightly spray four ¾-cup (185ml) capacity ovenproof dishes with oil. Line bases with baking paper. Place dishes on a baking tray.
2 Place dates and banana in a food processor and process until almost smooth. Add **NESTLÉ SOLEIL DIET Chocolate Mousse** and eggs and pulse until just combined. Transfer mixture to a medium bowl. Fold in flour.
3 Divide mixture among prepared dishes. Bake for 20–25 minutes or until firm to the touch. Stand puddings in dishes for 5 minutes before turning out onto serving plates. Heat topping in a small saucepan over low heat. Serve puddings drizzled with topping.
SERVE WITH: Low-fat custard. Add 1 *ProPoints* value per serve for ¼ cup (60ml).

YOU ONLY NEED A HANDFUL OF INGREDIENTS TO MAKE THESE INDULGENT PUDDINGS. COOKED IN INDIVIDUAL DISHES THEY ARE PORTION-PERFECT!

Berry crème with praline

 ProPoints VALUES PER SERVE | SERVES: 4 | PREP: 10 MINS | COOKING TIME: 15 MINS, PLUS 15 MINS COOLING

▲ **1 cup (220g) frozen raspberries**
**1 tbs caster sugar, plus ⅓ cup (75g)
extra for praline**
**2 x 125g tubs NESTLÉ SOLEIL DIET Crème
Caramel**
▲ **1 cup (240g) fat-free natural yoghurt**
3 tsp sesame seeds

*Filling & Healthy Foods are marked with a green triangle.
These foods help fill you up and keep you healthy.*

1 Place raspberries and 1 tablespoon sugar in a small
saucepan over medium heat. Bring to the boil. Reduce
heat to low and simmer, stirring occasionally, for
3–5 minutes or until thickened. Cool for 5 minutes.
Divide raspberry mixture among serving glasses.
2 Whisk both tubs of **NESTLÉ SOLEIL DIET Crème
Caramel** and yoghurt in a medium bowl until smooth.
Spoon caramel mixture over berries.
3 Line a baking tray with baking paper. Place extra ⅓ cup
(75g) sugar and 2 tablespoons water in a small non-stick
frying pan over medium-high heat. Cook, stirring, until
sugar dissolves. Bring to the boil. Boil, without stirring,
for 5 minutes or until golden. Pour onto prepared tray
and sprinkle with sesame seeds. Cool for 10 minutes or
until praline has set. Break into shards and sprinkle over
caramel mixture in glasses. Serve.

*TIP: You can use 1 tablespoon finely chopped toasted
almonds or pistachios instead of sesame seeds.
The **ProPoints** values remain the same.*

Strawberry roulade

 ProPoints VALUES PER SERVE | SERVES: 8 | PREP: 15 MINS, PLUS 30 MINS COOLING | COOKING TIME: 10 MINS

▲ **3 eggs**
½ cup (110g) caster sugar
¾ cup (105g) self-raising flour
1 cup (200g) reduced-fat fresh ricotta cheese
▲ **150g tub NESTLÉ SOLEIL DIET Vanilla Flavoured Yoghurt**
▲ **250g strawberries**
2 tsp icing sugar, to dust

Filling & Healthy Foods are marked with a green triangle. These foods help fill you up and keep you healthy.

1 Preheat oven to 200°C or 180°C fan-forced. Lightly spray a 25cm x 30cm Swiss roll tin with oil. Line tray with baking paper, allowing it to hang over the 2 long sides.
2 Using electric beaters, beat eggs and caster sugar in a small bowl for 3–4 minutes or until thick and creamy. Sift flour 3 times onto baking paper (see tip). Gently fold flour into egg mixture. Spread mixture evenly into tin. Bake for 8–10 minutes or until it springs back when lightly touched.
3 Meanwhile, place a piece of baking paper slightly larger than the tin on a flat surface. Turn cooked sponge immediately onto paper and peel off the lining paper. Trim crusty sides of sponge. Using the paper as a guide, roll sponge from 1 short side. Place onto a wire rack to cool.
4 Using electric beaters, beat ricotta and **NESTLÉ SOLEIL DIET Vanilla Flavoured Yoghurt** until almost smooth. Chop half the strawberries. Unroll sponge and spread with yoghurt mixture, leaving a 3cm border at both short ends. Sprinkle with chopped strawberries. Using the paper as a guide, re-roll sponge to enclose filling. Place roulade on a serving plate and dust with icing sugar. Serve with remaining strawberries.

TIP: *After sifting the flour onto baking paper, carefully pick up both long sides and use the paper to funnel the flour into the egg mixture.*

5 QUICK SNACK IDEAS

1 *Tomato & cheese cracker:* I Kavli Crispy Thin wholegrain crispbread, topped with I slice Bega So Extra Light 50% tasty cheese and sliced tomato.

2 *Tangy fruit salad:* I cup fruit salad (such as orange, passionfruit and strawberries) or half a small papaya, drizzled with juice of ½ a lime.

3 *Apple & cinnamon yoghurt:* I50g diet vanilla yoghurt, topped with chopped apple and a sprinkle of cinnamon.

4 *Sweet & spicy toast:* I slice wholegrain toast, topped with 2 tbs Weight Watchers Cottage Cheese, I tsp honey and I tsp dukkah (Middle Eastern nut and spice blend).

5 *Trail mix:* Combine IO raw, dry-roasted or smoked almonds, 2 tsp raw, roasted or tamari pepitas (pumpkin seed kernels) with I5g currants, sultanas, raisins or dried apricots.

| **2** *ProPoints* VALUES PER SERVE \| SERVES: 1 | **0** *ProPoints* VALUE PER SERVE \| SERVES: 1 | **2** *ProPoints* VALUES PER SERVE \| SERVES: 1 | **4** *ProPoints* VALUES PER SERVE \| SERVES: 1 | **4** *ProPoints* VALUES PER SERVE \| SERVES: 1 |

Snacks & treats

WHEN SHOULD I SNACK?

Always keep a range of healthy snacks on hand. Snacks can be a great addition to your daily meals and help us meet our recommended serves of **Filling & Healthy Foods**. Occasional treats also have a place. Listen to your body and choose your snacks and treats thoughtfully.

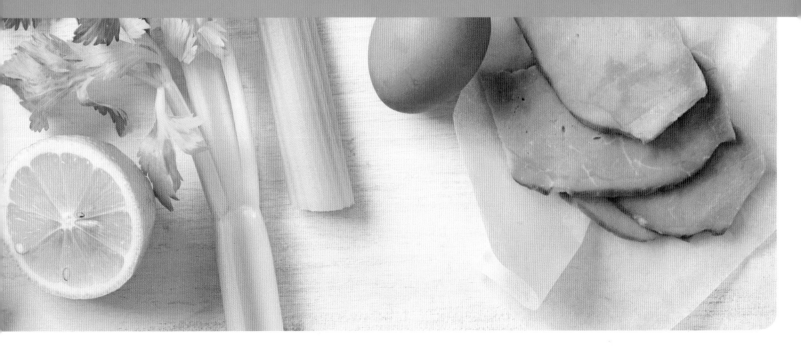

Bacon & corn polenta muffins

 ProPoints VALUE PER MUFFIN | MAKES: 24 | PREP: 15 MINS, PLUS 15 MINS STANDING TIME
COOKING: 20 MINS

▲ ¼ cup (40g) yellow polenta
▲ ⅓ cup (80ml) skim milk
   40g Weight Watchers Bacon,
      finely chopped
▲ 2 green shallots, finely chopped
   ¾ cup (110g) self-raising flour
▲ 125g can corn kernels, rinsed, drained
   125g can creamed corn
   ¼ cup (30g) Bega So Extra Light 50%
      grated cheese
   50g Weight Watchers Canola
      Spread, melted
▲ 1 egg, lightly beaten

*Filling & Healthy Foods are marked with a green triangle.
These foods help fill you up and keep you healthy.*

1 Preheat oven to 200°C or 180°C fan-forced. Line two 12-hole
(1 tablespoon/20ml) mini muffin tins with paper cases.
Combine polenta and milk in a bowl. Set aside for 15 minutes.
2 Meanwhile, lightly spray a small non-stick frying pan with
oil and heat over medium-high heat. Cook bacon, stirring, for
2 minutes. Add shallots and cook, stirring, for 2 minutes or
until bacon is crisp. Remove pan from heat. Cool for 5 minutes.
3 Sift flour into a large bowl. Add corn kernels, creamed corn,
cheese and bacon mixture and stir until combined. Add spread,
egg and polenta mixture and mix until just combined.
4 Spoon 1 tablespoon batter into each paper case. Bake for
12–15 minutes or until cooked when tested with a skewer.
Cool muffins in tins for 5 minutes before turning out onto a
wire rack. Serve warm or cold.

*TIP: Store muffins in an airtight container for up to 3 days.
Alternatively, cool completely then wrap individually in
plastic wrap and place in an airtight container. Label, date
and freeze for up to 1 month. Defrost at room temperature
and serve cold or warmed in the microwave.*

EASY AND QUICK TO MAKE, THESE
MOUTH-WATERING MINI MUFFINS DELIVER
A SATISFYING SAVOURY HIT AND ARE
TERRIFIC WARM OR COLD.

Spiced hommus with lavash chips

 ProPoints VALUES PER SERVE | SERVES: 4 | PREP: 15 MINS | COOKING TIME: 10 MINS

▲ **400g can chickpeas**
1 tbs tahini
1 tbs lemon juice
1 garlic clove, crushed
1 tsp ground cumin, plus extra to sprinkle
½ tsp allspice
2 x 55g pieces wholemeal lavash bread
Lemon wedges, to serve

*Filling & Healthy Foods are marked with a green triangle.
These foods help fill you up and keep you healthy.*

1 Rinse and drain chickpeas, reserving ¼ cup (60ml)
liquid. Place chickpeas and reserved liquid into a food
processor with tahini, juice and garlic.
2 Combine cumin and allspice in a small, dry, non-stick
frying pan over medium heat. Cook, stirring, for
30 seconds or until fragrant. Add to chickpea mixture
and process until smooth. Transfer hommus to a bowl.
3 Preheat oven to 180°C or 160°C fan-forced. Place lavash
on 2 baking trays. Bake for 6–8 minutes or until crisp. Cool.
Break into large shards. Sprinkle hommus with extra
cumin and serve with lavash chips and lemon wedges.

*TIP: Store lavash chips in an airtight container for
up to 2 weeks.*

Mango & lime smoothie

 ProPoints VALUES PER SERVE | SERVES: 2 | PREP: 10 MINS

▲ **1 mango, coarsely chopped (see tip)**
▲ **¾ cup (185ml) skim milk**
▲ **150g tub NESTLÉ SOLEIL DIET Vanilla Flavoured Yoghurt**
  1 tsp brown sugar
  1 tsp finely grated lime rind
  ½ cup ice cubes

Filling & Healthy Foods are marked with a green triangle. These foods help fill you up and keep you healthy.

1 Place mango, milk, yoghurt, sugar, rind and ice in a blender. Blend until smooth (see note).
2 Pour into glasses and serve immediately.
NOTE: Start blender on a low setting, then gradually increase the speed to high. This is easier on the motor and ensures ingredients are well combined.

TIP: To prepare mango, use a sharp knife to cut down either side of the stone to remove the 'cheeks'. Cut the flesh in a diamond pattern, then push the cheeks inside out and slice off the pieces of mango close to the skin.

Oat biscuits

ProPoints VALUE PER BISCUIT | **MAKES: 12** | **PREP: 15 MINS** | **COOKING TIME: 40 MINS**

▲ **1⅓ cups (120g) traditional rolled oats**
½ tsp salt
Pinch bicarbonate of soda
1 tsp finely chopped fresh rosemary
1 tbs olive oil

Filling & Healthy Foods are marked with a green triangle. These foods help fill you up and keep you healthy.

1 Preheat oven to 160°C or 140°C fan-forced. Line a baking tray with baking paper.
2 Combine oats, salt, bicarbonate of soda and rosemary in a mixing bowl. Season with freshly ground black pepper and make a well in the centre. Add oil and ⅓ cup (80ml) hot water and stir until well combined (mixture will become very sticky).
3 Turn mixture onto a piece of baking paper. Using wet hands, shape into a ball. Press dough out until 7mm thick. Using a 6cm round cutter, cut rounds from the dough. Press together any dough scraps and cut out more rounds to make 12 biscuits.
4 Place biscuits, 5cm apart, on prepared tray. Bake for 40–45 minutes or until crisp and golden. Cool on tray for 5 minutes before transferring to a wire rack to cool completely.
SERVE WITH: Bega So Extra Light 50% tasty cheese slices. Add 1 **ProPoints** value per serve for a 21g slice.

TIP: Store biscuits in an airtight container for up to 1 week.

Dried fig & oatmeal scones

3 *ProPoints* VALUES PER SCONE | MAKES: 16 | PREP: 25 MINS | COOKING TIME: 15 MINS

1²⁄₃ cups (250g) self-raising flour
½ cup (70g) fine oat bran, plus 1 tbs extra
   to sprinkle
2 tbs caster sugar
1½ tbs (30g) Weight Watchers Canola Spread
¾ cup (150g) finely chopped dried figs
1 cup (250ml) buttermilk (see note)
▲ 1 tbs skim milk

*Filling & Healthy Foods are marked with a green triangle.
These foods help fill you up and keep you healthy.*

1 Preheat oven to 220°C or 200°C fan-forced. Lightly spray a 19cm square cake tin with oil. Lightly dust with plain flour.
2 Sift self-raising flour into a large bowl. Stir in ½ cup (70g) oat bran and sugar. Using your fingertips, rub spread into flour mixture until it resembles breadcrumbs. Gently stir in fig and buttermilk until just combined. Lightly dust a flat surface with plain flour. Knead dough on floured surface for 30 seconds or until just smooth.
3 Press out dough until 2cm thick. Using a 5cm round cutter, cut 16 scones from dough. Arrange scones, just touching, in prepared tin. Brush lightly with skim milk and sprinkle with extra oat bran. Bake for 15–18 minutes or until scones are browned and sound hollow when tapped on the base. Serve hot or cold.
NOTE: Despite its name, buttermilk is low in fat. If unavailable you can use skim milk mixed with 1 teaspoon white vinegar or lemon juice.
SERVE WITH: Low-kilojoule fruit spread. Add 0 *ProPoints* value per serve for 1 tablespoon.

*TIP: You could use either ¾ cup (130g) sultanas, ¾ cup (110g) raisins or ¾ cup (110g) dried cranberries instead of dried figs. The **ProPoints** values remain the same.*

Raspberry buttermilk muffins

ProPoints VALUES PER MUFFIN | MAKES: 12 | PREP: 15 MINS | COOKING TIME: 20 MINS

2 cups (300g) self-raising flour
¼ cup (55g) caster sugar
1¼ cups (310ml) buttermilk (see note opposite)
▲ 1 egg
1 tsp vanilla essence
40g Weight Watchers Canola Spread, melted
▲ 1 cup frozen raspberries (see note)

Filling & Healthy Foods are marked with a green triangle.
These foods help fill you up and keep you healthy.

1 Preheat oven to 180°C or 160°C fan-forced. Line a 12-hole (⅓-cup/80ml capacity) muffin tin with paper cases.
2 Sift flour into a large bowl. Add sugar and stir to combine. Whisk buttermilk, egg, essence and spread in a medium bowl. Add to flour mixture and stir until just combined (don't overmix). Gently fold in raspberries.
3 Spoon mixture into paper cases. Bake for 20–25 minutes or until slightly risen and cooked when tested with a skewer. Cool muffins in tin for 5 minutes before turning out onto a wire rack to cool. Serve.
NOTE: Adding the raspberries while still frozen stops them 'bleeding' and staining the mixture when you fold them in.

TIP: These muffins are suitable to freeze. Cool completely, then wrap individually in plastic wrap and place in an airtight container. Label, date and freeze for up to 1 month. Defrost at room temperature and serve cold or warmed in the microwave.

Wholemeal pikelets

 ProPoints VALUE PER PIKELET | MAKES: 20 | PREP: 10 MINS | COOKING TIME: 15 MINS

1 cup (160g) wholemeal self-raising flour
Pinch salt
1 tbs caster sugar
▲ ¾ cup (185ml) skim milk
▲ 1 egg
1 tsp vanilla essence
½ cup (120g) extra-light cream cheese
½ cup (180g) diet maple syrup

Filling & Healthy Foods are marked with a green triangle. These foods help fill you up and keep you healthy.

1 Combine flour, salt and sugar in a medium bowl and make a well in the centre. Whisk milk, egg and essence in a jug until combined. Whisk egg mixture into flour mixture until just smooth.

2 Lightly spray a large non-stick frying pan with oil and heat over medium heat (see tip). Drop level tablespoons of batter into pan, allowing room to spread. Cook for 1–2 minutes or until bubbles appear on the surface. Turn and cook for 1–2 minutes or until golden. Transfer to a wire rack. Repeat with remaining batter to make 20 pikelets.

3 Spread warm or cold pikelets with cream cheese and drizzle with maple syrup. Serve.

TIP: Don't heat the pan too high, as pikelets need time to cook through before the outside gets too brown. Lightly spray the pan again as needed (move it away from the stovetop if cooking over a gas flame).

WITH A DAB OF CREAM CHEESE AND A DRIZZLE OF MAPLE SYRUP, THESE PETITE PIKELETS ARE PERFECT FOR AFTERNOON TEA OR A MID-MORNING TREAT.

Sesame toffees

 ProPoints VALUES PER TOFFEE | MAKES: 12 | PREP: 15 MINS | COOKING TIME: 15 MINS, PLUS 1 HOUR SETTING

2 tbs sesame seeds
1¼ cups (275g) caster sugar
1 tsp white vinegar
½ tsp cream of tartar (see note)

Filling & Healthy Foods are marked with a green triangle.
These foods help fill you up and keep you healthy.

1 Line a 12-hole (1 tablespoon/20ml capacity) mini muffin tin with squares of baking paper. Place sesame seeds in a small non-stick frying pan over medium heat. Cook, shaking, for 1–2 minutes or until lightly toasted.
2 Combine sugar, vinegar, cream of tartar and ½ cup (125ml) water in a saucepan over medium heat. Cook, stirring, until sugar dissolves. Bring to the boil. Reduce heat to low and simmer, without stirring, for 5–7 minutes or until light golden (be careful not to let the toffee become too brown, or it will taste burnt). Remove from heat. Set aside for 2 minutes or until bubbles subside.
3 Transfer toffee mixture to a heatproof jug. Carefully pour into prepared muffin holes. Sprinkle with sesame seeds. Set aside for 1 hour or until set.
NOTE: Cream of tartar helps stop crystals forming in the toffee, so it remains clear. The longer you cook the toffee mixture, the harder it will be when set.

TIP: Store toffees in an airtight container for up to 1 week.

Tomato & carrot soup

 0 | *ProPoints* VALUE PER SERVE | SERVES: 4 | PREP: 15 MINS | COOKING TIME: 35 MINUTES

▲ **1 brown onion, finely chopped**
▲ **1 carrot, chopped**
▲ **1 celery stick, chopped**
   1 garlic clove, crushed
▲ **1kg tomatoes, chopped**

Filling & Healthy Foods are marked with a green triangle. These foods help fill you up and keep you healthy.

1 Spray a large saucepan with oil and heat over medium-high heat. Add onion, carrot and celery and cook, stirring, for 5 minutes or until vegetables have softened. Add garlic and cook, stirring, for 30 seconds or until fragrant.
2 Add tomatoes and 2 cups (500ml) water and bring to the boil. Reduce heat to low and simmer for 20 minutes.
3 Using a stick blender or food processor, process soup until smooth. Return soup to low heat. Stir until heated through. Season with salt and freshly ground black pepper to serve.

TIP: This soup is suitable to freeze. Make double the recipe and ladle cooled soup into individual portion-sized airtight containers, leaving a 1–2cm gap at the top for expansion. Label, date and freeze for up to 2 months. Thaw in the fridge overnight before reheating in the microwave or a saucepan.

Banana & blueberry bread

 ProPoints VALUES PER SLICE | SERVES: 12 | PREP: 15 MINS | COOKING TIME: 1 HOUR

▲ **1 cup (240g) mashed banana (see note)**
▲ **125g fresh blueberries**
   ½ cup (110g) caster sugar
▲ **2 eggs, lightly beaten**
   ¼ cup (60ml) extra-light olive oil
▲ **¼ cup (60ml) skim milk**
   ¾ cup (120g) wholemeal self-raising flour
   ⅔ cup (100g) white self-raising flour

*Filling & Healthy Foods are marked with a green triangle.
These foods help fill you up and keep you healthy.*

1 Preheat oven to 190°C or 170°C fan-forced. Lightly spray a 22cm x 12cm (top measurement) loaf tin with oil. Line base and 2 long sides with baking paper, allowing paper to hang over the edges.

2 Combine banana, blueberries, sugar, egg, oil and milk in a large bowl. Sift flours into a large bowl. Return husks to bowl. Add flour mixture to banana mixture and stir until just combined.

3 Spoon mixture into prepared tin. Bake for 1 hour or until cooked when tested with a skewer. Stand bread in tin for 10 minutes before turning out onto a wire rack to cool. Cut into 12 even slices. Serve warm or cold.

NOTE: You will need 2 large ripe bananas.

SERVE WITH: Weight Watchers Canola Spread and maple syrup. Add 1 **ProPoints** value per serve for 1 teaspoon each of spread and maple syrup.

TIP: This bread is suitable to freeze. Wrap individual slices in plastic wrap and label, date and freeze for up to 2 months. Defrost at room temperature and serve cold or toasted.

OUR FRUIT-RICH VERSION OF A CAFE FAVOURITE SKIPS THE BUTTER BUT KEEPS THE FLAVOUR. IT WILL IMPRESS GUESTS AND IS A GREAT LUNCHBOX FILLER.

ProPoints
0
VALUE PER SERVING

- 1 orange (sliced), sprinkled with chilli flakes or chilli powder.

- 1 custard apple.

- ½ Lebanese cucumber (cut into wedges), mixed with a pinch of celery salt, 1 teaspoon chopped fresh dill, 2 tablespoons low-fat natural yoghurt and ¼ cup finely chopped fresh mint.

- 125ml tub Weight Watchers Jelly (any flavour).

- 1 tablespoon 0 *ProPoints* value tomato salsa with 0 *ProPoints* value vegetable sticks (carrot, cucumber and celery).

- 0 *ProPoints* value green salad, drizzled with fat-free dressing or balsamic vinegar.

- Shaved cucumber ribbons with chopped fresh dill and lemon juice.

- 1 cup blueberries.

- ½ punnet strawberries.

- 10 cherry tomatoes.

- 2 fresh dates.

- 1 cup cherries.

- 100g grapes.

- 0 *ProPoints* **value soup:** Cook 1 onion (finely chopped) and 1 red capsicum (finely chopped) in a medium saucepan (lightly sprayed with oil) until softened. Add 2 garlic cloves (crushed), 2 x 400g cans crushed tomatoes, 2 cups (500ml) vegetable stock and ¼ teaspoon chilli flakes (optional). Bring to the boil. Reduce heat and simmer for 5 minutes. Serve (blend with a stick blender if preferred).

Snack & treat ideas

Next time hunger calls, make sure you have a smart snack within easy reach. Whether you're at home, at work, shopping, exercising or just out and about, there are plenty of delicious, low *ProPoints* value snack options you can choose. Just plan ahead so you have the right ingredients, and take snacks with you when you head out the door so you're not caught empty-handed. We've listed some of our favourites for you to try.

ProPoints 1
VALUE PER SERVING

- 1 Kavli Crispy Thin wholegrain crispbread, topped with 1 slice Bega So Extra Light 50% cheese and sliced tomato.
- Fruit salad made with 1 banana (sliced), 6 strawberries (halved) and pulp of 1 passionfruit, drizzled with 1 teaspoon honey.
- Fruit salad made with 1 orange (sliced), 2 pitted fresh dates (chopped), pulp of 1 passionfruit, sprinkled with 1 tablespoon flaked almonds.
- 2 Vita-Weat crispbreads, topped with 1 teaspoon Vegemite and sliced tomato.
- 1 apple (sliced), topped with pieces from 1 slice Bega So Extra Light 50% cheese.
- 150g Weight Watchers Halved Apricots.
- 1 cup steamed vegetables, drizzled with 1 teaspoon flaxseed oil.
- 1 packet Continental Cup-a-Soup Classic Chicken Noodle.
- 1 cup air-popped popcorn.
- 2 dried pitted dates.
- 5 rice crackers with 1 tablespoon 0 **ProPoints** value tomato salsa.
- 1 cup miso soup.
- 1 water ice-block (any flavour).
- 135g tub Weight Watchers Fruit Snack, (any variety).
- 6 kalamata olives in brine.
- 2 tablespoons low-fat natural yoghurt.
- 2 teaspoons pepitas (pumpkin seed kernels) or sunflower seed kernels.
- 1 tablespoon mashed avocado with 0 **ProPoints** value vegetable sticks.
- 10 pistachio nuts.
- 150g diet yoghurt (any flavour).
- ½ packet Weight Watchers Fruities (any flavour).

ProPoints 2
VALUE PER SERVING

- 2 teaspoons reduced-fat peanut butter with celery sticks.
- 2 fresh figs, topped with 40g fresh ricotta cheese and 2 teaspoons honey.
- 125ml Weight Watchers Instant Dessert (any flavour).
- 1 cup 0 **ProPoints** value leftover roasted vegetables (such as carrot, red capsicum, zucchini, mushroom and onion), sprinkled with 1 tablespoon dukkah (Middle Eastern nut and spice blend).
- 2 Weight Watchers cookies (any variety).
- 2 fresh dates and 1 small (250ml) skim-milk cappuccino.
- 20g packet Carman's Muesli Bites (any flavour).
- 2 fresh dates (pitted), filled with 1 tablespoon Weight Watchers Cream Cheese.
- 150g diet yoghurt (any flavour), topped with 1 apple (chopped) and 5 raw almonds (chopped).
- 1 cup (250ml) canned minestrone soup, mixed with 100g steam fresh frozen vegetables (without corn or peas), microwaved.
- 1 Kavli Crispy Thin wholegrain crispbread, topped with 1 tablespoon Weight Watchers Cream Cheese, 30g sliced smoked salmon, a few baby capers in brine, slice of red onion and a squeeze of lemon juice.
- 2 tablespoons Weight Watchers Cream Cheese mixed with 2 teaspoons French onion soup mix. Serve with carrot sticks.
- 80g no-fat natural yoghurt, topped with 2 teaspoons honey and ½ cup thawed frozen berries.
- 19g packet Weight Watchers Nibblies (any flavour).
- 1 packet Continental Cup-a-Soup Asian Chinese Chicken & Corn.

- 1 apple (chopped), mixed with 4 walnut halves (chopped) and 60g Weight Watchers Cottage Cheese.
- 2 fresh dates (pitted), filled with 2 teaspoons tahini.
- **Hot 'choc-banana' smoothie:** Blend 1 cup (250ml) skim milk (heated) with 1 tablespoon cocoa powder and ½ banana.
- 2 corn or rice cakes with 1 tablespoon 0 **ProPoints** value tomato salsa.
- 6 dried apricot halves.
- 95g can tuna in springwater with 0 **ProPoints** value salad.
- 20g packet Weight Watchers Potato Bakes (any flavour).
- 1 small (250ml) skim-milk cappuccino or latte.
- 5 pieces dried apple.
- 40g Weis Mango and Cream mini bar.
- 105g Streets Calippo ice-block (any flavour).
- 1 Weight Watchers Drinking Chocolate made following packet instructions with 200ml hot water.
- 1 slice fruit bread, spread with 1 tablespoon diet jam.
- 2 rice cakes.
- 25g Weight Watchers Choc Crisp bar.
- ½ punnet strawberries with 62g tub diet chocolate mousse.
- 1 milkshake made with 1 cup (250ml) skim milk and 1 tablespoon diet topping.

- 2 Vita-Weat crispbreads, spread with 2 teaspoons Vegemite and 60g Weight Watchers Cottage Cheese.

- 2 rice thins, spread with 2 teaspoons ABC (almond, Brazil, cashew nut) spread.

- 1 tablespoon tahini served with carrot sticks.

- 150g tub low-fat natural yoghurt, mixed with 1 teaspoon honey, 1 banana (sliced) and ¼ teaspoon ground cinnamon.

- 2 tablespoons low-fat baba ganoush, mixed with 2 tablespoons Weight Watchers Cottage Cheese and 1 green shallot (finely chopped). Serve with 0 **ProPoints** value vegetable sticks (carrot, cucumber and capsicum).

- 1½ cups air-popped popcorn, sprinkled with 1 teaspoon Mexican, Moroccan, lamb or lemon pepper seasoning.

- 150g tub diet yoghurt (any flavour), topped with 2 tablespoons natural muesli and ¼ cup thawed frozen raspberries.

- 1 cup miso soup (made with instant sachet and boiling water), poured over 50g shelf-fresh udon noodles and ½ cup finely shredded baby spinach leaves.

- 2 Vita-Weat crispbreads, topped with sliced tomato, 20g baby bocconcini cheese (sliced) and fresh basil leaves, drizzled with 1 teaspoon balsamic vinegar.

- 1 corn thin, topped with 30g Weight Watchers Cottage Cheese, 1 teaspoon chopped fresh chives, 30g sliced smoked salmon and a squeeze of lemon juice.

- **Turkey & cranberry rolls:** Spread 3 slices (90g) roast turkey with 2 teaspoons cranberry sauce. Top with 3 tablespoons grated carrot. Roll to eat.

- 3 dried apricots and 2 Brazil nuts.

- 1 slice wholegrain bread, spread with 15g Weight Watchers Apricot Fruit Spread.

- 1 hard-boiled egg (sliced) and 1 wholegrain Ryvita crispbread (any variety), topped with sliced tomato and 2 slices (20g) Weight Watchers Ham.

- 2 Ryvita crispbreads (any type), topped with 4 slices (40g) Weight Watchers Ham and 1 tomato (sliced).

- 80g no-fat natural yoghurt, topped with 2 teaspoons honey and 2 teaspoons LSA (linseed, sunflower seed, almond) mix.

- 1 wholegrain wrap, filled with 2 slices (20g) Weight Watchers Ham, lettuce and 0 **ProPoints** value vegetable sticks.

- 1 Ryvita crispbread (any variety), topped with 30g fresh ricotta cheese, 1 fresh date (pitted, chopped) and 2 walnut halves (chopped).

- 1 sachet Jarrah 99% fat-free Chocolatte drink made following packet instructions with 1 cup (250ml) skim milk.

- 1 Weight Watchers Fruit Cereal Bar (any flavour).

- 1 tablespoon avocado with 2 corn or rice cakes.

- 200g low-fat natural yoghurt.

- 1 (120g) corn on the cob.

- 1 slice wholegrain toast, spread with 1 tablespoon diet jam.

- 2 Ryvita multigrain crispbreads, topped with 2 tablespoons low-fat cottage cheese.

- 30g traditional rolled oats cooked with water.

- 1 slice wholegrain bread, spread with 1 tablespoon low-fat hommus.

- 16 raw almonds.

- 130g can Weight Watchers Baked Beans.

- 10 banana chips.

- 15 rice crackers.

ProPoints™

4

VALUE PER SERVING

- 30g Uncle Tobys Chewy Muesli Bar (apricot).

- 25g bhuja mix (Indian savoury nibble mix).

- 30g roasted chickpeas.

- 1 piece mountain bread, topped with 1 tablespoon Weight Watchers Cream Cheese and freshly grilled capsicum, mushroom and zucchini.

- 1 Weight Watchers Drinking Chocolate made following packet instructions with 200ml skim milk.

- 1 Ryvita crispbread (any variety), topped with 2 teaspoons quince paste, 30g sliced smoked salmon and 20g avocado (sliced).

- 2 Kavli Crispy Thin wholegrain crispbreads, topped with 85g can tuna in springwater (drained), mixed with 1 green shallot (finely chopped), 2 teaspoons chopped fresh parsley leaves, 2 gherkins (chopped) and 1 tablespoon Weight Watchers Mayonnaise.

- 1 hard-boiled egg, sprinkled with 1 tablespoon dukkah.

- 5 rice crackers, topped with 2 tablespoons Weight Watchers Cream Cheese, 1 tablespoon grated carrot and 2 teaspoons sultanas.

- 100g 97% fat-free honey yoghurt, topped with 1 banana (sliced) and 1 tablespoon toasted flaked almonds.

- 1 Ryvita crispbread (any variety), topped with ½ tin (35g) sardines.

- ½ tub (125g) Weight Watchers Cottage Cheese, mixed with 1 apple (chopped) and 1 tablespoon sultanas.

- ½ wholegrain wrap, spread with 1 teaspoon harissa (North African chilli paste) and filled with 20g baby bocconcini cheese (sliced) and 2 artichokes in brine (sliced).

- 2 Ryvita crispbreads (any variety), topped with 2 tablespoons low-fat hommus.

- 1 rice cake, topped with 2 teaspoons tahini and 1 teaspoon honey.

- ½ English muffin, topped with 25g slice lean ham and 1 slice Bega So Extra Light 50% cheese. Grill until cheese has melted.

- 1 small (47g) low-fat muffin.

- 6 pieces (90g) sushi roll (no avocado or fried fillings).

- 25 unsalted roasted peanuts.

- 1 boiled egg with 1 slice wholegrain toast.

- 1 regular (42g) plain scone, spread with 2 teaspoons berry jam.

- 30g Sanitarium Organic Mix Fruit and Nut.

Kitchen essentials

The kitchen is the hub of any home and is also likely to be at the centre of your healthy eating. The simple choices you make about how to cook your food and how to stock your pantry, fridge and freezer will help you to confidently plan your meals and lose weight.

See our Cooking basics guide (p154) for the equipment that will get you cooking with less fat and ensure your portions are correct. But first up it's the food you shop for and have on hand in your kitchen that will get you cooking and eating for weight loss, health and enjoyment. By keeping a good selection of staples on hand it's always easy to whip up a satisfying meal or healthy snack when you don't have time to get to the supermarket. Here's our basic checklist to get you started.

Fridge basics

It's easy to end up with a fridge full of rarely used sauces and drooping vegetables. For food safety, keep the temperature constant – don't overstock your fridge and place foods with a shorter fridge-life (such as yoghurt) towards the front so you remember to use them. When storing food, make sure it's well covered to keep odours at a minimum, and put cooked food above raw food to minimise the risk of cross-contamination. Empty your fridge regularly and wipe down surfaces with some fresh-smelling vanilla essence. Before placing food back in, discard anything that's past its use-by date or is unlikely to be used before it goes off.

FRIDGE CHECKLIST

FRIDGE	FREEZER
■ **EGGS.**	■ **CHICKEN BREAST FILLETS.**
■ **CHEESE** – parmesan (for pasta), low-fat ricotta, Weight Watchers Cottage Cheese, reduced-fat feta, and Bega So Extra Light 50% tasty.	■ **FISH FILLETS** – such as snapper, ling and blue-eye trevalla.
■ **FRESH HERBS.**	■ **FROZEN BERRIES.**
■ **LEAN BACON.**	■ **FROZEN VEGETABLES** – such as beans, peas, broccoli and cauliflower.
■ **LEAN DELI MEATS** – such as chicken, ham and turkey breast.	■ **LEAN RED MEAT** – beef, lamb and pork (fat trimmed) and mince.
■ **LOW-FAT YOGHURT AND SOUR CREAM.**	■ **READY-MADE PASTRY** – filo and reduced-fat puff and shortcrust.
■ **SEASONAL FRUIT AND VEGETABLES.**	■ **WEIGHT WATCHERS FROZEN MEALS** – for convenience and portion control.
■ **SKIM AND LOW-FAT MILK** – or soy and grain substitutes, such as rice or oat milk.	■ **WEIGHT WATCHERS ICE CREAM.**
■ **TOFU** – firm tofu is best for stir-fries and soups.	■ **WHOLEGRAIN BREAD AND ROLLS.**

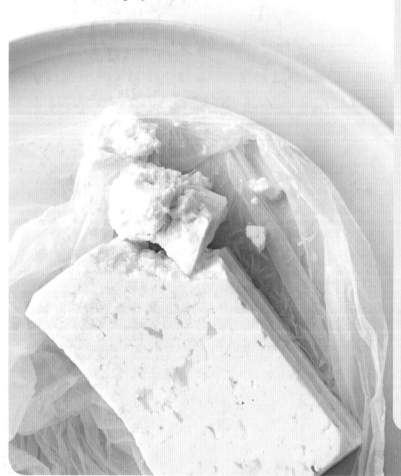

Recipe index

Measurements

SECRETS TO RECIPE SUCCESS

To achieve the same results as seen in this book, please note:

- We used eggs with an average weight of 59g.
- We used standard metric measuring equipment approved by Standards Australia. This includes:

1 A 250 millilitre jug for measuring liquids.

2 A graduated set of four measuring cups (1 cup, ½ cup, ⅓ cup and ¼ cup) for measuring dry ingredients such as flour, sugar etc.

3 A graduated set of four measuring spoons (1 tablespoon, 1 teaspoon, ½ teaspoon and ¼ teaspoon) for small liquid and dry ingredients. Be aware that while Australian, New Zealand, UK and USA teaspoons all have 5ml capacity, only Australian tablespoons are 20ml. New Zealand, USA and UK tablespoons are only 15ml, which could make a difference to the **ProPoints** values.

- All spoon and cup measurements are level (for dry ingredients, use a knife to level off along the edge).

OVEN TEMPERATURES

	CONVECTION	FAN-FORCED
Very slow	120°C	100°C
Slow	150°C	130°C
Moderately slow	160–170°C	140–150°C
Moderate	180–200°C	160–180°C
Moderately hot	210–230°C	190–210°C
Hot	240–250°C	220–230°C
Very hot	260°C	240°C

Senior Food Editor: Lucy Kelly
Assistant Food Editor: Cathie Lonnie
Photography: Rob Palmer
Styling: Marie-Hélène Clauzon, Lisa Featherby
Food Preparation: Lucy Busuttil, Nick Banbury
Recipe Development: Peta Dent, Cathie Lonnie, Sally Parker, Kirrily la Rosa, Tracy Rutherford
Food Content Manager: Kristine Iligan
Food Content Administrator: Nour Nahza
Advertising & Publishing Coordinator: Yara Oulabi
Nutrition Communications Managers: Roslyn Anderson, Ana Riberio
National Corporate Advertising Manager: Marion Sheehan
Director Publishing & Programme: Kate Cody

Weight Watchers Australia:
Locked Bag 2020,
Broadway NSW 2007
Phone: 13 19 97
www.weightwatchers.com.au

Weight Watchers NZ:
PO Box 1328, Auckland.
Phone: 0800 009 009
www.weightwatchers.co.nz

Copyright © 2012 Weight Watchers International, Inc. All Rights Reserved.

Published by ACP Magazines Limited, under arrangement with Weight Watchers International, Inc.
Produced by ACP Custom Media, a division of ACP Magazines Ltd
Level 18, 66-68 Goulburn Street, Sydney 2000
Phone: (02) 9282 8000
Fax: (02) 9267 3625
Editor: Tracey Platt
Art Director: Sally Keane
Copy Editors: Kyle Rankin, Mark Bradridge
Production Coordinator: Rachel Walsh
Prepress Team Leader: Peter Suchecki

ACP Corporate
Managing Director ACP Magazines: Phil Scott
Publishing Director ACP Magazines: Gerry Reynolds

ACP Custom Media
General Manager: Sally Wright
Publishing Manager: Nicola O'Hanlon

Nine Entertainment Co.
Chief Executive Officer: David Gyngell
Group Sales and Marketing Director: Peter Wiltshire

Printed by Toppan Printing Co, China.

Our new name means 'sunshine'.

You'll think it means fresher, thicker, better taste.

We've changed our name from Nestle Diet to Soleil (sol-lay). Our new name comes with a fresher, thicker taste too. Don't worry though, we're still no fat and low in sugar.*

Start your day sunny side up